学ぶ人は、
変えて
ゆく人だ。

目の前にある問題はもちろん、

人生の問いや、

社会の課題を自ら見つけ、

挑み続けるために、人は学ぶ。

「学び」で、

少しずつ世界は変えてゆける。

いつでも、どこでも、誰でも、

学ぶことができる世の中へ。

旺文社

JN247494

全レベル問題集
英語長文

駿台予備学校講師 三浦淳一 著

3

私大標準レベル

改訂版

はじめに

　大学受験に向けた英語学習は，書店の学習参考書コーナーに行けばすぐにわかるとおり，とても細分化されています。単語・熟語，文法・語法，構文，英作文，長文読解，リスニング，会話表現，発音・アクセント…

　これを1つずつやっていたら，何年かかっても終わりそうにありません。

　「一石二鳥」という言葉がありますが，短期間で英語の学習を仕上げるには，いわば「一石五鳥」「一石六鳥」の学習をすることです。つまり，1つの学習で複数の効果を得られるような学習をすべきなのです。

　『大学入試 全レベル問題集　英語長文』シリーズは，長文読解の問題集という形をとっていますが，これにとどまらず，語彙力をつけたり，重要な文法事項の確認をしたり，音声を用いた学習により，発音・アクセント，リスニングの力をつけることも目指しています。

　本シリーズはレベル別に6段階で構成されており，必ず自分にピッタリ合った1冊があるはずです。また，現時点の実力と志望校のレベルにギャップがあるなら，1～2段階レベルを下げて，英語力を基礎から鍛え直すのもおすすめです。受験生はもちろん，高校1・2年生からスタートすることもできます。

　本シリーズは最新の大学入試問題の傾向に対応し，さらに，英語4技能（Reading / Listening / Writing / Speaking）を今後ますます重視する入試制度にも対応しうる，本質的・普遍的な英語力をつけることを目的にしています。

　本シリーズを利用して，皆さんが第一志望の大学に合格することはもちろん，その先，一生の武器となる確固たる英語力を身につけてほしいと願っています。

三浦　淳一

目　次

音声について

本書の英文を読み上げた音声を，専用ウェブサイト・スマートフォンアプリで聞くことができます。英文ごとに，2種類の音声を収録しています。全文通し読みの音声と，段落ごとに区切ったややゆっくりめの音声があります。段落ごとに区切った音声は，ディクテーションでご利用ください。 01 のように示しています。

●ウェブサイトで聞く方法
・以下のサイトにアクセスし，パスワードを入力してください。
　https://www.obunsha.co.jp/service/zenlevel/
　※すべて半角英字。検索エンジンの「検索欄」は不可。
　パスワード：zlchoubunt
・右上の QR コードからもアクセスできます。

●スマートフォンアプリで聞く方法
・音声をスマートフォンアプリ「英語の友」で聞くことができます。「英語の友」で検索するか，右下の QR コードからアクセスしてください。
・パスワードを求められたら，上と同じパスワードを入力してください。

⚠ご注意ください　◆音声を再生する際の通信料にご注意ください。◆音声は MP3 形式となっています。音声の再生には MP3 を再生できる機器などが別途必要です。デジタルオーディオプレーヤーなどの機器への音声ファイルの転送方法は，各製品の取り扱い説明書などをご覧ください。ご使用機器，音声再生ソフトなどに関する技術的なご質問は，ハードメーカーもしくはソフトメーカーにお問い合わせください。◆スマートフォンやタブレットでは音声をダウンロードできないことがあります。◆本サービスは予告なく終了することがあります。

本シリーズの特長

大学入試 全レベル問題集 英語長文」シリーズには，以下の特長があります。

1. 細かく分かれたレベル設定

本シリーズはレベル別からなる6冊で構成されており，学習者の皆さんそれぞれがベストな1冊を選んで大学入試対策をスタートできるようにしています。各書がレベルに応じた収録英文数と設問構成になっています。

2. 語彙力を重視

語彙力は語学学習における基本です。単語がわからなければ英文を読むにも書くにも不自由します。本書ではオールラウンドな語彙力をつけられるよう，幅広いテーマの英文を選びました。各ユニットの最後に，語句リストの復習（ミニテスト）や，音声を利用した単語のディクテーション問題を設け，語彙力が増強できるよう工夫しています。

3. 英文構造の明示

すべての英文の構造を示し（SVOC分析），英文を完全に理解できるようにしました。さらに，本文の和訳例も，あまり意訳をせず，文構造を反映させた直訳に近い日本語にしました。

4. 文法事項のわかりやすい解説

近年の入試問題では，難関大学を中心に文法問題の出題が減少しており，「文法問題を解くための文法学習」は，もはや時代遅れです。本書では「英文を正しく読むための文法」を心がけて解説しています。

5. 設問の的確な解説

すべての設問に，なるべく短く的確な解説をつけました。特に本文の内容に関する設問は，根拠となる箇所を明示して解説しています。類書と比較しても，わかりやすく論理的な解説にしています。これは，解説を読んで納得してほしいということもありますが，それ以上に，読者の皆さんが自分で問題を解くときにも，このように論理的に考えて，正解を導き出せるようになってほしいからです。

6. 音声による学習

付属の音声には本書に掲載した英文の音声が2パターンで収録されています。主にリスニング力UPを目的としたナチュラルに近いスピードのものは，シャドーイング*1 やオーバーラッピング*2 用です。また1つ1つの単語の発音がわかるようなややゆっくりしたスピードのものは，ディクテーション問題用です。

> *1 シャドーイング・・・すぐ後から音声を追いかけて，同じ内容を口に出す練習方法
> *2 オーバーラッピング・・・流れてくる音声とぴったり重なるように口に出す練習方法

著者紹介：**三浦淳一**（みうら じゅんいち）

早稲田大学文学部卒。現在，駿台予備学校・医学部受験専門予備校 YMS 講師。『全国大学入試問題正解 英語』（旺文社）解答・解説執筆者。『入門 英語長文問題精講 [3訂版]』『医学部の英語』（以上，旺文社），『センター英語 英語[語句整序] を 10 時間で攻略する本』『世界一覚えやすい中学英語の基本文例 100』（以上，KADOKAWA）ほか著書多数。「N 予備校」「学びエイド」などで映像授業も担当する。

〔協力各氏・各社〕

装丁デザイン：ライトパブリシティ 録音・編集：ユニバ合同会社
本文デザイン：イイタカデザイン ナレーション：Ann Slater, Guy Perryman, Katie Adler
  編集担当：高杉健太郎

志望校レベルと「全レベル問題集 英語長文」シリーズのレベル対応表

＊ 掲載の大学名は本シリーズを活用していただく際の目安です。

本書のレベル	各レベルの該当大学
① 基礎レベル	高校基礎～大学受験準備
② 共通テストレベル	共通テストレベル
③ 私大標準レベル	日本大学・東洋大学・駒澤大学・専修大学・京都産業大学・近畿大学・甲南大学・龍谷大学・札幌大学・亜細亜大学・國學院大學・東京電機大学・武蔵大学・神奈川大学・愛知大学・東海大学・名城大学・追手門学院大学・神戸学院大学・広島国際大学・松山大学・福岡大学 他
④ 私大上位レベル	学習院大学・明治大学・青山学院大学・立教大学・中央大学・法政大学・芝浦工業大学・成城大学・成蹊大学・津田塾大学・東京理科大学・日本女子大学・明治学院大学・獨協大学・北里大学・南山大学・関西外国語大学・西南学院大学 他
⑤ 私大最難関レベル	早稲田大学・慶應義塾大学・上智大学・関西大学・関西学院大学・同志社大学・立命館大学 他
⑥ 国公立大レベル	北海道大学・東北大学・東京大学・一橋大学・東京工業大学・名古屋大学・京都大学・大阪大学・神戸大学・広島大学・九州大学 他

本書で使用している記号一覧

Check! …………… 文法事項の説明

🔊 …………… 音声番号

SVOC解析

S, V, O, C ……… 主節における文の要素

S, V, O, C ……… 従属節における文の要素

S′, V′, O′, C′ …… 意味上の関係を表す文の要素

① ② ③ ………… 並列関係にある要素

〈　　〉………… 名詞句, 名詞節

〔　　〕………… 形容詞句, 形容詞節

（　　）………… 副詞句, 副詞節

関代 ………… 関係代名詞

関副 ………… 関係副詞

等接 ………… 等位接続詞

従接 ………… 従属接続詞

疑 ………… 疑問詞

… so ～ that … 相関語句

語句リスト

動 …………… 動詞

名 …………… 名詞

形 …………… 形容詞

副 …………… 副詞

接 …………… 接続詞

関 …………… 関係詞

前 …………… 前置詞

熟 …………… 熟語

志望大学別 入試長文分析と学習アドバイス

大学名	日本大学	東洋大学	駒澤大学
英文レベル※	★2.0 　1-----2-----3-----4	★2.1 　1-----2-----3-----4	★1.9 　1-----2-----3-----4
出題ジャンル	 社会 4.0% 科学・技術 4.0% 産業 4.0% 自然 12.0% 文化 48.0% 日常生活 28.0%	 日常生活 10.0% 社会 10.0% 科学・技術 10.0% 自然 40.0% 文化 30.0%	 社会 15.4% 文化 53.8% 日常生活 30.8%
	長文問題の平均出題大問数 **2.5 問**	長文問題の平均出題大問数 **2.0 問**	長文問題の平均出題大問数 **2.6 問**
	長文1題あたり平均語数 **418 語**	長文1題あたり平均語数 **580 語**	長文1題あたり平均語数 **283 語**
設問形式	☑内容一致（選択式） ☐内容一致（T or F） ☑空所補充 ☐下線部言い換え ☑表題選択 ☐下線部和訳 ☐記述説明 ☐その他	☑内容一致（選択式） ☑内容一致（T or F） ☑空所補充 ☑下線部言い換え ☐表題選択 ☐下線部和訳 ☐記述説明 ☑その他	☑内容一致（選択式） ☐内容一致（T or F） ☑空所補充 ☐下線部言い換え ☐表題選択 ☐下線部和訳 ☐記述説明 ☑その他
三浦先生Check!	基本的に記述問題は出題されていない。段落ごとの内容を問う問題が中心。大問の1つが内容一致問題，もう1つが空所補充問題。	空所補充は文法問題。内容真偽判定問題が中心。英文は日常生活に関するテーマなど，わかりやすいものが多い。	英文が短く，設問は内容一致問題が中心で，取り組みやすい。文系学部のみの大学だが，英文のテーマは自然科学系が多い。

※T or F：内容真偽判定問題

＊英文レベル ＝ 1：基礎　2：共通テストレベル　3：やや難　4：難

専修大学

★2.0

1……2……3……4

- 産業 10.0%
- 社会 10.0%
- 自然 10.0%
- 文化 30.0%
- 日常生活 40.0%

長文問題の平均出題大問数
2.0 問

長文1題あたり平均語数
626 語

- ☑ 内容一致（選択式）
- ☐ 内容一致（T or F）
- ☑ 空所補充
- ☑ 下線部言い換え
- ☑ 表題選択
- ☐ 下線部和訳
- ☐ 記述説明
- ☑ その他

難解な語句が含まれる英文を出すが，語注が多いので理解の妨げにはならない。用法識別や文法力を重視する空所補充問題が目立つ。

京都産業大学

★2.0

1……2……3……4

- 産業 20.0%
- 社会 20.0%
- 文化 20.0%
- 日常生活 40.0%

長文問題の平均出題大問数
2.0 問

長文1題あたり平均語数
369 語

- ☑ 内容一致（選択式）
- ☐ 内容一致（T or F）
- ☑ 空所補充
- ☐ 下線部言い換え
- ☑ 表題選択
- ☐ 下線部和訳
- ☐ 記述説明
- ☐ その他

空所補充と内容一致のシンプルな出題形式。内容一致問題は事前に設問に目を通すことがポイント。英文の内容は具体的でわかりやすい。

近畿大学

★1.9

1……2……3……4

- 文化 10.0%
- 日常生活 10.0%
- 科学・技術 10.0%
- 社会 20.0%
- 自然 20.0%
- 産業 30.0%

長文問題の平均出題大問数
2.0 問

長文1題あたり平均語数
260 語

- ☑ 内容一致（選択式）
- ☐ 内容一致（T or F）
- ☑ 空所補充
- ☑ 下線部言い換え
- ☐ 表題選択
- ☐ 下線部和訳
- ☐ 記述説明
- ☐ その他

空所補充と内容一致のシンプルな出題形式。英文はあまり長くなく，読みやすい。内容一致問題を正確に解くことがポイントになる。

	甲南大学	龍谷大学	札幌大学
英文レベル※	★1.9 1 — 2 — 3 — 4	★1.9 1 — 2 — 3 — 4	★1.8 1 — 2 — 3 — 4
出題ジャンル	科学・技術 3.3% 産業 6.7% 自然 6.7% 社会 13.3% 日常生活 36.7% 文化 33.3%	日常生活 10.0% 自然 20.0% 文化 70.0%	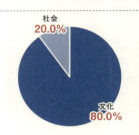社会 20.0% 文化 80.0%
	長文問題の平均出題大問数 **3.0 問**	長文問題の平均出題大問数 **2.0 問**	長文問題の平均出題大問数 **1.0 問**
	長文1題あたり平均語数 **447 語**	長文1題あたり平均語数 **628 語**	長文1題あたり平均語数 **632 語**
設問形式	☑ 内容一致（選択式） ☐ 内容一致（T or F） ☑ 空所補充 ☑ 下線部言い換え ☐ 表題選択 ☑ 下線部和訳 ☐ 記述説明 ☑ その他	☑ 内容一致（選択式） ☐ 内容一致（T or F） ☑ 空所補充 ☑ 下線部言い換え ☑ 表題選択 ☐ 下線部和訳 ☐ 記述説明 ☑ その他	☑ 内容一致（選択式） ☑ 内容一致（T or F） ☑ 空所補充 ☐ 下線部言い換え ☐ 表題選択 ☑ 下線部和訳 ☑ 記述説明 ☑ その他
三浦先生Check!	段落ごとに内容理解を問う問題が中心で，他は単語・熟語の知識問題。文系学部は和訳問題があるので対策が必要。	文中に十数カ所もの下線があり，細かく理解を問う設問。段落ごとに設問を処理するのが効率的。英文の内容は平易。	和訳，説明問題などが出題され，記述力が問われる。英文のテーマは歴史などに関するものが多い。

※T or F：内容真偽判定問題

亜細亜大学	神奈川大学	東京経済大学

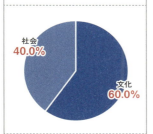

社会 40.0%
文化 60.0%

日常生活 7.1%
社会 14.3%
文化 28.6%
自然 14.3%
科学・技術 14.3%
産業 21.4%

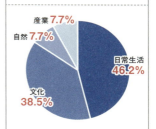

産業 7.7%
自然 7.7%
日常生活 46.2%
文化 38.5%

長文問題の平均出題大問数	長文問題の平均出題大問数	長文問題の平均出題大問数
1.7 問	**2.6 問**	**2.6 問**

長文1題あたり平均語数	長文1題あたり平均語数	長文1題あたり平均語数
481 語	**448 語**	**415 語**

亜細亜大学	神奈川大学	東京経済大学
☑ 内容一致（選択式）	☑ 内容一致（選択式）	☑ 内容一致（選択式）
☐ 内容一致（T or F）	☐ 内容一致（T or F）	☐ 内容一致（T or F）
☑ 空所補充	☐ 空所補充	☑ 空所補充
☐ 下線部言い換え	☑ 下線部言い換え	☐ 下線部言い換え
☐ 表題選択	☐ 表題選択	☑ 表題選択
☐ 下線部和訳	☐ 下線部和訳	☐ 下線部和訳
☐ 記述説明	☐ 記述説明	☐ 記述説明
☑ その他	☐ その他	☐ その他

英文を段落ごとに区切って内容を問う問題が中心で, 他の問題は年により空所補充, 下線部言い換えなど。

基本的に下線部言い換えと内容一致のみ。内容一致問題はあらかじめ問いに目を通しておくと効果的。

空所補充と内容一致が中心。語注が多いので, 語彙力が弱くても内容を理解できる。英文のテーマは幅広い。

大学名	愛知大学	中京大学	名城大学
英文レベル※	★1.8 1……2……3……4	★1.8 1……2……3……4	★1.9 1……2……3……4
出題ジャンル	産業 12.5% 日常生活 50.0% 文化 37.5%	自然 14.3% 日常生活 28.6% 文化 57.1%	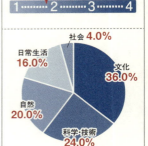社会 4.0% 日常生活 16.0% 文化 36.0% 自然 20.0% 科学・技術 24.0%
	長文問題の平均出題大問数 **2.0 問**	長文問題の平均出題大問数 **2.3 問**	長文問題の平均出題大問数 **2.1 問**
	長文1題あたり平均語数 **662 語**	長文1題あたり平均語数 **345 語**	長文1題あたり平均語数 **526 語**
設問形式	☑ 内容一致（選択式） ☐ 内容一致（T or F） ☑ 空所補充 ☑ 下線部言い換え ☑ 表題選択 ☑ 下線部和訳 ☑ 記述説明 ☑ その他	☑ 内容一致（選択式） ☐ 内容一致（T or F） ☑ 空所補充 ☑ 下線部言い換え ☐ 表題選択 ☐ 下線部和訳 ☐ 記述説明 ☑ その他	☑ 内容一致（選択式） ☐ 内容一致（T or F） ☑ 空所補充 ☑ 下線部言い換え ☑ 表題選択 ☐ 下線部和訳 ☐ 記述説明 ☑ その他
三浦先生Check!	比較的短めの英文に，指示語や用法識別など細かい設問が多く出題される。短い記述説明や下線部和訳もあり，記述力も求められる。	空所補充，内容一致，下線部分言い換え問題がバランス良く出題される。グラフ問題は慣れが必要。	文系学部は一般的な内容一致・空所補充問題。理系学部はこれに加え，文整序や文補充問題もあり，慣れが必要。

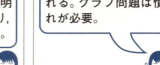

※T or F：内容真偽判定問題

10

追手門学院大学

⭐ 1.5
1 ……… 2 ……… 3 ……… 4

社会 12.5%
日常生活 37.5%
産業 25.0%
自然 25.0%

長文問題の平均出題大問数
2.0 問

長文1題あたり平均語数
398 語

☑ 内容一致（選択式）
☐ 内容一致（T or F）
☑ 空所補充
☑ 下線部言い換え
☑ 表題選択
☐ 下線部和訳
☐ 記述説明
☐ その他

> 内容一致と空所補充が中心。英文は短めでわかりやすい内容のものが多い。内容一致問題は丁寧に解けば全問正解を狙える。

神戸学院大学

⭐ 1.8
1 ……… 2 ……… 3 ……… 4

自然 11.1%
科学・技術 11.1%
文化 33.3%
産業 22.2%
日常生活 22.2%

長文問題の平均出題大問数
1.8 問

長文1題あたり平均語数
437 語

☑ 内容一致（選択式）
☐ 内容一致（T or F）
☑ 空所補充
☑ 下線部言い換え
☐ 表題選択
☐ 下線部和訳
☐ 記述説明
☑ その他

> 出題形式は，空所補充，下線部の言い換え，内容一致などさまざま。「正しくないもの」を選ばせる問題が多いので注意。

本データに記載の内容は，『2016 年受験用 全国大学入試問題正解 英語』〜『2020 年〃』を旺文社編集部が独自に分析したものです。ただし，亜細亜大，中京大は『2016 年〃』〜『2018 年〃』の分析結果です。

英文を読むための基礎知識

英文を読む上で，単語や熟語の知識が必要なのは当然である。しかし，語句の意味がわかれば英文を正しく理解できるというわけではない。英文は日本語とは異なる「構造」を持っているので，「構造」を把握することが英文を読むときには不可欠だ。

文型と文の要素

(1) 文型とは，英語の文のパターンを分類したものだ。英語の文には5つの文型があるとされている。

第1文型：	S + V
第2文型：	S + V + C
第3文型：	S + V + O
第4文型：	S + V + O + O
第5文型：	S + V + O + C

(2) そして，文型を構成する1つ1つのパーツのことを，文の要素と呼んでいる。これも5つある。

S	（主語）	：「～は」「～が」と訳す。**名詞**。
V	（述語）	：「～する」「～である」と訳す。**動詞**。
O	（目的語）	：「～を」「～に」と訳す。**名詞**。
C	（補語）	：決まった訳し方はない。**名詞**または**形容詞**。
M	（修飾語）	：決まった訳し方はない。**形容詞**または**副詞**。

句と節

「句」も「節」も，2語以上のカタマリを意味するが，以下のような違いがある。

「句」→〈S+V〉を含まないカタマリ。 「節」→〈S+V〉を含むカタマリ

1. 句

(1) 名詞句

S, O, C になる句。**不定詞や動名詞のカタマリ**である。どちらも，「**～すること**」と訳す場合が多い。

例 My desire is 〈to study abroad〉. 「私の希望は留学することだ」
　　 S　　　 V C

(2) 形容詞句

名詞を修飾する句。**不定詞，分詞，前置詞のカタマリ**がこれにあたる。

例 I have a lot of *homework* 〔to do〕. 「私にはやるべき宿題がたくさんある」
　 S　 V　　　　　 O

(3) 副詞句

名詞以外（主に動詞）を修飾する句。**不定詞，分詞，前置詞のカタマリ**がこれにあたる。なお，分詞が副詞句を作ると，「分詞構文」と呼ばれ，【時】【理由】【付帯状況】などの意味を表す。

例 He *went* to America (to study jazz). 「彼はジャズの研究をするためにアメリカへ行った」
　 S　 V

to study jazz という不定詞のカタマリが went という動詞を修飾している。【目的】「～するために」

例 He *entered* the room, (taking off his hat). 「彼は帽子を脱ぎながら部屋に入った」
　 S　 V

taking off his hat という分詞のカタマリ（分詞構文）が entered という動詞を修飾している。
【付帯状況】「～しながら」

例 I *got* (to the station) (at ten). 「私は10時に駅に到着した」
　 S　 V

to the station と at ten という2つの前置詞のカタマリが，いずれも got という動詞を修飾している。

2. 節

（1）名詞節

S, O, C になる節。①従属接続詞（that / if / whether），②疑問詞，③関係詞が名詞節を作る。

① 従属接続詞は，節を作るタイプの接続詞だ。そして，従属接続詞は数多くあるが，その中で**名詞節を作れるのは that「…こと」／ if「…かどうか」／ whether「…かどうか」の3つだけ**で，それ以外のすべての従属接続詞は副詞節しかない。

例 〈**That** you study Spanish now〉 is a good idea.
　　　S　　S　　V　　　O　　　　　V　C

「あなたが今スペイン語を勉強する**こと**はいい考えだ」

例 I don't know 〈**if**[**whether**] he will come here tomorrow〉.
　　　S　　V　　O　　　　　　　　　　S　　V

「明日彼がここに来るの**かどうか**わからない」

② 疑問詞も名詞節を作る。

例 I don't know 〈**what** he wants〉.　　「私は，彼が**何を**欲しがっている**のか**知らない」
　　　S　　V　　O　　　　　S　　V

③ **一部の関係詞も名詞節を作る**ことがある。これは，関係詞の中では少数派であり，関係詞の大半は，次に見る形容詞節を作る。名詞節を作る関係詞は，**what「…すること／…するもの」**と **how「…する方法」**を押さえておこう。

例 〈**What** I want〉 is a new car.　　「私が欲しい**もの**は新しい車だ」
　　　S　　　S　V　　V　C

例 This is 〈**how** I solved the problem〉.
　　　S　V　C　　　　S　　V　　　O

「これが，私が問題を解決した**方法**だ（→このようにして私は問題を解決した）」

（2）形容詞節

名詞を修飾する働きをする節。これを作るのは**関係詞**だけだ。

例 I have *a friend* 〔**who** lives in Osaka〕.　　「私には大阪に住んでいる友人がいる」
　　　S　V　　O　　　　　　　V

関係代名詞 who から始まるカタマリが friend という名詞を修飾。

例 This is *the place* 〔**where** I met her first〕.「ここは私が初めて彼女に会った場所だ」
　　　S　V　　C　　　　　　　S　V　O

関係副詞 where から始まるカタマリが place という名詞を修飾。

（3）副詞節

名詞以外（主に動詞）を修飾する節。従属接続詞は全て，副詞節を作ることができる。

例 I like him （**because** he is generous）.　　「彼は気前がいいので好きだ」
　　　S　V　O　　　　　　　　S　V　C

従属接続詞 because から始まるカタマリが like という動詞を修飾している。

＊ 先ほど名詞節のところで出てきた that / if / whether は，名詞節だけではなく副詞節も作ることができる（ただし，that は so 〜 that … 構文など，特殊な構文に限られる）。**if** は「もし…すれば」，**whether** は「…しようがするまいが」の意味では副詞節である。

例 I will stay home （**if** it rains tomorrow）.　「もし明日雨が降ったら，家にいるつもりだ」
　　　S　　V　　　　　　　S　　V

従属接続詞 if から始まるカタマリが stay という動詞を修飾している。

このほか，「複合関係詞」と呼ばれる特殊な関係詞が副詞節を作ることができる。

例 I will reject your offer （**whatever** you say）.「たとえ君が何を言っても，私は君の申し出を断ります」
　　　S　　V　　　O　　　　　　　　S　V

※ さらに詳しい解説は，本シリーズのレベル①（p.6〜15），レベル②（p.6〜19）を参照して下さい。

解 答

| 問 | （ア） ② | （イ） ① | （ウ） ④ | （エ） ④ | （オ） ③ |

解 説

問

（ア）「ローマ帝国時代から中世まで」

① 「寿命が大幅に延びた」

② **「寿命はわずかしか延びなかった」**

③ 「寿命はまったく延びなかった」

④ 「寿命はわずかに縮んだ」

▶ 第1段落第3文参照。本文の only a little を選択肢②では only a slight と言い換えている。

（イ）「中世には」

① **「黒死病で人口の4分の1が死亡した」**

② 「医療が多くの人々の恐ろしい病気を治癒した」

③ 「死に至る病気でヨーロッパの人口が半減した」

④ 「飢饉はめったに起こらなかった」

▶ 第1段落最終文参照。本文の a quarter を選択肢①では one fourth と言い換えている。

（ウ）「産業革命は」

① 「黒死病の主たる原因であった」

② 「イングランドの急激な人口減少の原因となった」

③ 「人間の寿命が劇的に延びた後に始まった」

④ **「寿命の着実な伸長より前に起こった」**

▶ 第2段落第1文参照。なお，A follow B で「A は B の後に続く，B は A に先行する」の意味になり，この受動態が B is followed by A である。

（エ）「平均寿命は」

① 「ヨーロッパではここ数世紀，延びが止まっている」

14

② 「19 世紀以来，最長寿国では変化していない」

③ 「ヨーロッパでは毎年，3 カ月ずつ縮んでいる」

④ **「最長寿国では毎年 3 カ月ずつ延びている」**

▶ 第 2 段落第 2 文参照。

(オ) 「この文章のタイトルとなりうるのは」

① 「中世の生活」

② 「産業革命と人口」

③ **「寿命の延び」**

④ 「病気と寿命」

▶ 「中世」「病気」は第 1 段落，「産業革命」は第 2 段落にしか記述がない。第 1 段落，第 2 段落を通じて一貫して焦点が当たっているのは「寿命の延び」である。

▼

それでは次に，段落ごとに詳しくみていこう。 01

第 1 段落　文の構造と語句のチェック

強調構文

¹It's (only in very recent history) that we've been able to dream of 〈 living
　　　　　　　　　　　　　　　　　　　　　S　　　　V　　　　　　　　O

long, active lives 〉.　²(During the Roman Empire), life span was just 22 years.
　　　　　　　　　　　　　　　　　　　　　　　　　　S　　　V　　　C

³(By the Middle Ages in England), (some 1,500 years later), there was
　　　　　　　　　　　　　　　　　　　　　　　　　　　　　　　　　　　　V

only a little improvement — people could expect to live (about 33 years), and
　　　　　　　　　　　　S　　　　S　　　　　V　　　　　　　　　　　　　　　　等接

could 省略　　　expect to live 省略
not necessarily (healthy years) either.　⁴The threat of famine was ever-present,
　　　　　　　　　　　　　　　　　　　　　　　　　　　　　S　　　　V　　　C

and medicine was limited (to a few brutal surgical techniques).　⁵Plagues often
等接　　S　　　V　　　　　　　　　　　　　　　　　　　　　　　　　　　　　S

occurred, and the Black Death, 〔 which swept (through Europe) (between 1347
   V   等接   S   関代   V

and 1351)〕, killed a quarter of the population.
              V   O

訳 ¹歴史上ごく最近になってやっと，長く元気に生きることを夢見ることが可能になってきた。²ローマ帝国時代，寿命はわずか 22 年だった。³約 1,500 年後の中世のイングランドでも，わずかな改善しかなかった。人々は約 33 年しか生きることを期待できなかったし，必ずしも健康な年月を生きられるわけでもなかったのだ。⁴飢饉の脅威は常に存在し，医療は少数の荒っぽい外科技術に限られていた。⁵疫病が頻繁に発生し，1347 年から 1351 年にかけてヨーロッパ中に広まった黒死病により人口の 4 分の 1 が亡くなった。

Check! 　第 3 文 By the Middle Ages in England, some 1,500 years later, … の挿入句の some 1,500 years later は the Middle Ages を言い換えている。カンマにはこのように言い換えの働きがある。some は数字の前に置かれると「およそ，約」の意味の副詞。

語 句

recent	形	最近の	limit *A* to *B*	熟	A を B に限る，限定する
active	形	活発な	brutal	形	荒々しい，残忍な
life span	名	寿命	surgical	形	外科(手術)の
some	副	およそ，約	technique	名	技術
improvement	名	改善，向上，伸び	plague	名	疫病，伝染病
expect	動	期待する	occur	動	起こる，発生する
not necessarily	熟	必ずしも～ない	the Black Death	名	黒死病
either	副	(否定文で)～もまた(ない)	sweep	動	急速に広まる
threat	名	脅威，おそれ	＊活用：sweep-swept-swept		
famine	名	飢饉，食料不足	quarter	名	4 分の 1
ever-present	形	絶えず存在する	population	名	人口
medicine	名	医療，医術			

第2段落　文の構造と語句のチェック

¹The dramatic improvement 〔 in human life span 〕 didn't start (until the Industrial Revolution), which began (in England) (in the 19th century) and
　S　　　　　　　　　　　　　　　　　　　　　　　　V　　　　　　　　　　　　　　　　　　　　　　　　　　　　　　関代　V①　　　　　　　　　　　　　　　　　　　　　等接

spread quickly (throughout Europe). ²(Since 1840), the average life span 〔 in
V②　　　　　　　　　　　　　　　　　　　　　　　　　　　　　　　　　　　　S

the longest-lived countries 〕 has improved steadily — (rising by three months
　　　　　　　　　　　　　　　　　　　V

every year). ³And that growth continues (to this day).
　　　　　　　　　　等接　　　　S　　　　　　V

> 訳 ¹人間の寿命の劇的な改善は，19世紀にイングランドで始まって急速にヨーロッパ中に広まった産業革命が起こってようやく開始した。²1840年以来，最長寿国の平均寿命は，着実に延びており，毎年3カ月ずつ長くなっている。³そしてその伸長が今日に至るまで続いている。

Check! 第1文 The dramatic improvement in human life span didn't start until the Industrial Revolution … の not 〜 until … は，直訳すれば「…まで〜ない」だが，「…してはじめて〜する，…になってやっと〜する」などと訳すことが多い。

語句

dramatic	形	劇的な	long-lived	形	長寿の
spread	動	広まる	improve	動	改善する，向上する
quickly	副	素早く，急速に	steadily	副	着実に
throughout	前	〜のいたる所に，〜の隅から隅まで	rise	動	上昇する
			growth	名	増加，高まり，成長
average	形	平均的な	continue	動	続く
			to this day	熟	今日まで

文法事項の整理 ①　強調構文

第1段落第1文の It's ～ that ... についてみてみよう。

It's only in very recent history **that** we've been able to dream of living long, active lives.

　これは【強調構文】で，It is ～ that ... の「～」の部分を強調する表現である。基本的には**「…するのは～だ」**と訳すが，「～こそ…する，まさに～が…する」などの訳し方も可。

例　My brother bought a new car last month.
　　　　①　　　　　　　②　　　　　　③

（①を強調）　It was <u>my brother</u> that bought a new car last month.
　　　　　　　　　　　　　　[who]
　　　　　　　「先月新車を買ったのは私の兄だ」

（②を強調）　It was <u>a new car</u> that my brother bought last month.
　　　　　　　「私の兄が先月買ったのは新車だ」

（③を強調）　It was <u>last month</u> that my brother bought a new car.
　　　　　　　「私の兄が新車を買ったのは先月だ」

It is ～ that ... の形は形式主語構文の場合もあるので，区別に注意しよう。

■ It is ～ that ... の識別方法（＊It の指示対象が前にない場合）

～ が形容詞		形式主語構文
～ が名詞	... が完全な文	
	... が不完全な文	強調構文
～ が副詞		
～ が〈前置詞＋名詞〉		

　本文の It's only in very recent history that we've been able to dream of living long, active lives. は，It's と that の間に〈前置詞＋名詞〉の副詞句が挟まっているので，強調構文とわかる。なお，〈only＋時点を表す語句〉は「～になってやっと，～してはじめて」などと訳す。

語句リストの復習

次の語句の意味を**ア〜ト**からそれぞれ１つ選べ。

/20点

1	life span	11	spread
2	quarter	12	quickly
3	improvement	13	improve
4	medicine	14	continue
5	expect	15	occur
6	technique	16	famine
7	threat	17	plague
8	steadily	18	rise
9	population	19	average
10	dramatic	20	recent

ア	４分の１	サ	医療
イ	平均的な	シ	飢饉
ウ	期待する	ス	脅威
エ	人口	セ	改善
オ	広まる	ソ	劇的な
カ	着実に	タ	最近の
キ	素早く	チ	上昇する
ク	技術	ツ	改善する
ケ	起こる	テ	寿命
コ	疫病	ト	続く

答 　1－テ　2－ア　3－セ　4－サ　5－ウ　6－ク　7－ス　8－カ　9－エ　10－ソ
　　11－オ　12－キ　13－ツ　14－ト　15－ケ　16－シ　17－コ　18－チ　19－イ　20－タ

今回学習した英文に出てきた単語を，音声を聞いて（　　　）に書き取ろう。

It's only in very **❶**(r　　　　　) history that we've been able to dream of living long, active lives. During the Roman Empire, life span was just 22 years. By the Middle Ages in England, some 1,500 years later, there was only a little **❷**(i　　　　　　) — people could expect to live about 33 years, and not necessarily healthy years either. The threat of famine was ever-present, and **❸**(m　　　　　) was limited to a few brutal surgical techniques. Plagues often occurred, and the Black Death, which swept through Europe between 1347 and 1351, killed a **❹**(q　　　　　) of the population.

The dramatic improvement in human life span didn't start until the Industrial Revolution, which began in England in the 19th century and **❺**(s　　　　) quickly throughout Europe. Since 1840, the **❻**(a　　　　) life span in the longest-lived countries has improved steadily — rising by three months every year. And that growth **❼**(c　　　　) to this day.

答 **❶** recent　**❷** improvement　**❸** medicine　**❹** quarter　**❺** spread　**❻** average
❼ continues

解答

問	(ア) ②	(イ) ①	(ウ) ①	(エ) ④	(オ) ③

解説

問

(ア) 【存在】を表す with。**with the exception of ~** で「~を例外として，~という例外はあるが」の意味。

(イ) ① **wherever** は「どこで…しても」の意味で，文意に合う。② however「どんなに[どのように]…しても」は文意に合わない。③ whenever については，文末に at the end of the day という時を表す語句があるのに，whenever「いつ…しても」では意味的に無理がある。④ whoever は後に不完全な文(SやOの欠けた文)が続くので文法的に不可。

(ウ) **the same ~ as S+V** で「S が V するのと同じ~」の意味。

(エ) ① for は等位接続詞で「というのは…だからだ」の意味があるが，ここでは前後の因果関係は不明なので不可。② that は接続詞の場合，名詞節を導いて「…ということ」の意味だが，ここでは空所以下がなくても文が成立する(OやCなどの名詞要素の欠落はない)ことから，名詞節とは考えられない。③ unless は「…しない限り」の意味で副詞節だが，意味的に不可。④ **while** は【時】【譲歩】のほか，「…する一方で，他方で…」の【対比】の意味を持ち，これが文意に合う。

(オ) 「火を使って」の意味で【付帯状況】を表す分詞構文と考え，現在分詞の③ Using を選ぶ。① Use だと原形なので命令文になるが，この後に接続詞がなく S＋V が続いているので不可。② To use だと「火を使うために」と【目的】の意味になるが，内容として不自然。④ Used は分詞構文で【受動】を表す過去分詞と考えれば fire という O が続かないはずだし，過去形と考えても S がない点がおかしい。

第１段落　文の構造と語句のチェック

¹A vast stretch of land lies untouched (by civilization) (in the back country
　　　　S　　　　　　　V　　C

[of the eastern portion [of the African continent]]). ²(With the occasional

exception of a big-animal hunter), foreigners never enter this area. ³(Aside
　　　　　　　　　　　　　　　　　S　　　　　V　　O

from the Wandorobo tribe), even the natives stay away (from this particular
　　　　　　　　　　　　　　　S　　　　V

area) (because it is the home [of the deadly tsetse fly]). ⁴The tribe depend on
　　　　　　従接　S V　　C　　　　　　　　　　　　　　　　S　　　V

the forest (for their lives), ①(eating its roots and fruits) and ②(making
O　　　　　　　　　　　　　　　　　V′　　O′　　　　等接　　　V′

their homes (wherever they find themselves (at the end of the day))).
O′　　　　　　従接　　S　　V　　O

　　　　　　　　　┌── 関代 which 省略
⁵One of the things [they usually eat] is honey. ⁶They obtain it (through an
　S　　　　　　　　S　　　　V　　　V　C　　　S　　　V　O

ancient, symbiotic relationship [with a bird [known as the Indicator]]).

⁷The scientific community finally confirmed the report ⟨ that this bird
　S　　　　　　　　　　　　　　　V　　　　　　　O　　　　従接(同格)　S

intentionally led the natives to trees [containing the honey of wild bees]]⟩.
　　　　　　V　　O

⁸Other species of honey guides are also known (to take advantage of
　S　　　　　　　　　　　V　　　　　　　　V′

the search efforts of some animals (in much the same way [as the Indicator
O′　　　　　　　　　　　　　　　　　　　　　　　　　　　　関代　S

22

$$\underset{V}{\text{uses}}\ \underset{O}{\text{men}}\ ])).$$

訳 ¹アフリカ大陸東部の奥地に広大に広がる土地が，文明から手つかずの状態で残っている。²大型動物を求めるハンターという時折の例外はありつつ，外国人はこの地域にまったく入らない。³ワンドロボ族を除けば，原住民でさえこの特別な地域には近づかない。なぜなら，そこは死をもたらすツェツェバエの生息地だからだ。⁴ワンドロボ族は生活を森林に依存しており，その根や果実を食べ，一日の終わりにはどこにいようとも，その場所に家を作る。⁵彼らが普段食べるものの1つがハチミツである。⁶彼らは，インディケーター（指示する者）として知られる鳥との昔からの共生関係を通じてハチミツを手に入れる。⁷科学界はついに，この鳥が意図的に原住民を野生のミツバチのハチミツを含む樹木に案内しているという報告の裏付けをとった。⁸他の種のハチミツ案内役も，このインディケーターが人間を利用するのとほとんど同じ方法で，動物たちがハチミツを探す労力を利用していることが知られている。

Check! 第7文の The scientific community finally confirmed the report that this bird intentionally led the natives to trees containing the honey of wild bees. の that は【同格】の接続詞で，that 以下が直前の report の具体的内容を説明している。

語句

vast	形	広大な
stretch	名	広がり，一帯
lie	動	～のままである
＊活用：lie-lay-lain		
untouched	形	手つかずの，未開発の
civilization	名	文明
back country	名	奥地，僻地，未開地
eastern	形	東の
portion	名	部分
continent	名	大陸
occasional	形	時たまの，時々の
exception	名	例外
hunter	名	ハンター，狩人
foreigner	名	外国人
enter	動	入る
area	名	地域，地方
aside from ~	熟	～は別として，～以外に
tribe	名	部族
native	名	原住民，現地人
stay away from ~	熟	～に近づかない，～を避ける
particular	形	特別な
home	名	生息地
deadly	形	死を招く
depend on *A* for *B*	熟	A に B を頼る，B のために A に依存する
forest	名	森林，山林
root	名	（植物の）根
wherever	接	どこで…しても
at the end of ~	熟	～の終わりに
honey	名	ハチミツ
obtain	動	手に入れる
ancient	形	古い，昔からの
relationship	名	関係
indicator	名	指示する者，指標，標識

scientific	形	科学の，科学的な		bee	名	ミツバチ
community	名	共同体，～界		species	名	種，種類
confirm	動	確証する，裏付ける		guide	名	案内役，ガイド
intentionally	副	わざと，意図的に		take advantage of ~	熟	～を利用する
lead *A* to *B*	熟	A を B に導く，案内する		search	名	探求，捜索
contain	動	含む		effort	名	苦労，作業，活動，努力
wild	形	野生の		much the same ~	熟	ほぼ同じ～

第2段落　文の構造と語句のチェック

¹This amazing bird settles (in a tree 〔 near a Wandorobo camp 〕) and sings
S　　　　　　　V①　　　　　　　　　　　　　　　　　　　　　等接　V②

incessantly (until the men answer it (with whistles)). ²It then begins
　　　　　　　　従接　S　　V　　O　　　　　　　　　　　　S　　　　V

its leading flight. ³Singing, it hops (from tree to tree), (while the men continue
O　　　　　　　　　　　S　V　　　　　　　　　　　従接　S　　V

their musical answering call). ⁴(When the bird reaches the tree), its voice
O　　　　　　　　　　　　　　従接　S　　　V　　O　　　　　S

becomes shriller and its followers examine the tree carefully. ⁵The Indicator
V　　　C　　等接　S　　　　　V　　　O　　　　　　　　　　S

usually sits (just over the bees' nests), and the men hear the sounds 〔 of the
　　　V　　　　　　　　　　　　　　　　　等接　S　　V　　O

bees 〔 in the hollow trunk 〕〕. ⁶(Using fire), they smoke most of the bees (out of
　　　　　　　　　　　　　　　　　V′　O′　S　　V　　O

the bees
‖

the tree), but those 〔 that escape the effects of the smoke 〕 attack the men
等接　S　　関代　V　　　　O　　　　　　　　　　　V　　　O

violently. ⁷(In spite of the attack), the Wandorobos, gather the honey and
　　　　　　　　　　　　　　　　　S　　　　　V①　　O　　　等接

leave a small gift (for their bird guide).
V②　　O

訳 ¹この驚くべき鳥はワンドロボ族の野営地の近くにある樹木に住みつき，人間が口笛で応答するまで絶え間なく鳴く。²そして，案内飛行を開始するのだ。³人間が音楽を奏でるように口笛で応答している間，この鳥はさえずりながら木から木へと跳んで行く。⁴鳥が（ハチミツのとれる）木に着くと，声がさらに甲高くなり，後をつけてきた人間はその木を注意深く確認する。⁵インディケーターはたいていミツバチの巣の真上に止まり，そのとき人間には幹の空洞にいるミツバチの音が聞こえる。⁶火を利用して，人間はミツバチのほとんどを木からいぶし出すのだが，煙の影響を逃れたミツバチは人間に激しく攻撃を仕掛ける。⁷その攻撃にもかかわらず，ワンドロボ族はハチミツを集め，案内係の鳥に少々のプレゼントを残していくのである。

語句

amazing	形	驚くべき，驚異的な
settle	動	定住する
camp	名	野営(地)，キャンプ(場)
whistle	名	口笛
flight	名	飛ぶこと，飛行
hop	動	ぴょんぴょんと跳ぶ
follower	名	後をつける者
examine	動	確かめる，確認する
nest	名	巣
smoke	動	いぶし出す，（煙で）追い出す
escape	動	逃れる，免れる
effect	名	影響
violently	副	激しく，乱暴に
in spite of ~	熟	～にもかかわらず
gather	動	集める
leave	動	残す

文法事項の整理 ②　分詞構文

第 1 段落第 4 文の eating ... making ... についてみてみよう。

The tribe depend on the forest for their lives, **eating** its roots and fruits and **making** their homes wherever they find themselves at the end of the day.

　これは【**分詞構文**】で，分詞構文とは分詞（現在分詞，過去分詞）が副詞の働きをすることである。

　分詞構文は【**時**】【**理由**】【**条件**】【**譲歩**】など，様々な意味を表すことができる。

■分詞構文の表す意味

①【時】「〜するときに」

例　**Walking** across the street, I met an old friend of mine.
「道を歩いているときに私は旧友に会った」

②【理由】「〜するので」

例　**Written** in easy English, this book is suitable for beginners.
「易しい英語で書かれているので，この本は初心者に適している」

③【条件】「もし〜すれば」

例　**Born** in better days, he could have succeeded.
「もっといい時代に生まれていれば，彼は成功できたのだが」

④【譲歩】「〜だけれど」

例　**Admitting** what you say, I can't support you.
「あなたの言うことは認めるが，あなたを支援することはできない」

⑤【付帯状況】「〜しながら」

例　**Taking** off his hat, he entered the room.
「彼は帽子を脱ぎながら部屋に入った」

※分詞構文が文の後半(S＋Vより後)に出てくる場合は【付帯状況】を表すことが多い。「～しながら，～して，～したまま，そして～する」などと訳す。

> 例　He entered the room, **taking** off his hat.
> 「彼は帽子を脱ぎながら部屋に入った」
> 「彼は部屋に入り，そして帽子を脱いだ」

(第1段落第4文)

The tribe depend on the forest for their lives, <u>eating</u> its roots and fruits and <u>making</u> their homes wherever they find themselves at the end of the day.

▶ eating と making が並列されており，いずれも【付帯状況】を表す分詞構文。「～して，～しながら」などと訳す。

(第2段落第3文)

<u>Singing</u>, it hops from tree to tree, while the men continue their musical answering call.

▶ Singing は現在分詞で，【付帯状況】を表す分詞構文。

(第2段落第6文)

<u>Using</u> fire, they smoke most of the bees out of the tree, but those that escape the effects of the smoke attack the men violently.

▶ Using は現在分詞で，【付帯状況】を表す分詞構文。

語句リストの復習

次の語句の意味を**ア**～**ト**からそれぞれ1つ選べ。

/20点

1 civilization	**12** amazing	
2 intentionally	**13** nest	
3 continent	**14** in spite of ～	
4 obtain	**15** scientific	
5 exception	**16** stay away	
6 ancient	from ～	
7 aside from ～	**17** indicator	
8 effect	**18** violently	
9 contain	**19** settle	
10 species	**20** vast	
11 take advantage		
of ～		

ア 大陸		**サ** ～を利用する
イ 文明		**シ** 種（しゅ）
ウ ～は別として		**ス** 手に入れる
エ 広大な		**セ** 影響
オ ～に近づかない		**ソ** ～にもかかわらず
カ 含む		**タ** 巣
キ わざと		**チ** 定住する
ク 古い，古代の		**ツ** 例外
ケ 指標		**テ** 激しく，乱暴に
コ 科学の		**ト** 驚くべき

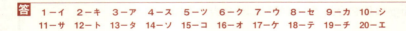

答　1－イ　2－キ　3－ア　4－ス　5－ツ　6－ク　7－ウ　8－セ　9－カ　10－シ
11－サ　12－ト　13－タ　14－ソ　15－コ　16－オ　17－ケ　18－テ　19－チ　20－エ

ディクテーションしてみよう！ 🔊 05-06

今回学習した英文に出てきた単語を，音声を聞いて（　　　）に書き取ろう。

　A vast stretch of land lies untouched by **❶**(c 　　　　　　) in the back country of the eastern portion of the African **❷**(c 　　　　　　). With the occasional exception of a big-animal hunter, foreigners never enter this area. Aside from the Wandorobo tribe, even the natives stay away from this particular area because it is the home of the deadly tsetse fly. The tribe depend on the forest for their lives, eating its roots and fruits and making their homes wherever they find themselves at the end of the day. One of the things they usually eat is honey. They **❸**(o 　　　　　　) it through an ancient, symbiotic relationship with a bird known as the Indicator. The **❹**(s 　　　　　　) community finally confirmed the report that this bird intentionally led the natives to trees containing the honey of wild bees. Other species of honey guides are also known to take **❺**(a 　　　　　　) of the search efforts of some animals in much the same way as the Indicator uses men.

　This amazing bird **❻**(s 　　　　　　) in a tree near a Wandorobo camp and sings incessantly until the men answer it with whistles. It then begins its leading flight. Singing, it hops from tree to tree, while the men continue their musical answering call. When the bird reaches the tree, its voice becomes shriller and its followers examine the tree carefully. The Indicator usually sits just over the bees' **❼**(n 　　　　　), and the men hear the sounds of the bees in the hollow trunk. Using fire, they smoke most of the bees out of the tree, but those that escape the **❽**(e 　　　　) of the smoke attack the men violently. In **❾**(s 　　　　) of the attack, the Wandorobos gather the honey and leave a small gift for their bird guide.

答 **❶** civilization　**❷** continent　**❸** obtain　**❹** scientific　**❺** advantage　**❻** settles　**❼** nests
❽ effects　**❾** spite

解答

問1	②	問2	③	問3	①	問4	②
問5	④	問6	④	問7	③, ④, ⑤		

解説

問1

fast は「断食する」の意味の動詞。意味を知らなくても，文頭にある【逆接】を表す However「しかし」の働きや，第1段落第1文の stop eating が主題を提示している点に注目すれば，推測は可能。

問2

空所直前の前置詞 in と合わせて各選択肢の意味を検討すると，① in turn「順番に，同様に」，② in detail「詳細に」，③ in protest「抗議して」，④ in competition「競争して」となる。第2段落第2文で女性に投票権がなかったこと，空所を含む第2段落第3文では女性による断食の実行について書かれているので，③が正解。

問3

justice は「公平，公正」の意味で，**否定の接頭辞 in- が付いた injustice は「不公平，不公正」の意味**になる。また，this は前出の内容（多くは直前の文に含まれる）を指す。ここでは，第2段落第2文の内容（女性に投票権が認められていなかったこと）を指していると考えれば，injustice の語義と合う。

問4

接続詞 as は【時】【理由】【様態】【比例】などの意味を持つが，【様態】「…するように，…するとおりに」の意味の場合，本文のように as 以下で倒置が起こり，〈as＋ be[do / have など]＋ S〉の語順になることがある。【様態】の as は主節と従属節の内容が共通していることを示す。

　例　John is very clever, **as** *is* his brother.
　　　「ジョンは，彼の兄がそうであるように，非常に賢い」
ここでの do の内容は，「ヒンドゥー教徒」との共通点を挙げている文脈なの

で，fast on special occasion を指すと考えるべき。よって②が正解。

問5

　各選択肢の意味は，①「食べ物」，②「よく売れるもの，販売者」，③「場所」，④「薬」。直後の2文で，断食をすることで風邪や発熱がなくなったとあるので，④が適切。

問6

　本文で一貫して論じられているのは「断食の理由」である。第1段落は主題を提示し，第2段落は政治的理由による断食，第3段落は宗教的理由による断食，第4段落は健康上の理由による断食について述べられている。したがって，④「食べ物なしで済ませる理由」が正解。

問7

① 「私たちは余分なカロリーを身体にため込まないためには身体的に活発でなくてはならない」

▶ そのような記述はない。

② 「モーハンダース・ガンジーは政治的な手段として断食をしたのではない」

▶ 第2段落第6文と不一致。

③ 「**セザール・チャベスは政治的理由により断食をした**」

▶ 第2段落第9～12文と一致。なお，第2段落第1文に for political reasons とあるので，この段落の3つの具体例はいずれも政治的理由と考えてよい。

④ 「**マーク・トウェインは断食が風邪を治す有効な方法だと思っていた**」

▶ 第4段落第3～5文と一致。

⑤ 「**アプトン・シンクレアはかつて，たくさん食べて，胃の不調に苦しんだ**」

▶ 第4段落第6文と一致。

⑥ 「今日では人々はもう断食をしない」

▶ 第1段落第3文，第2段落第1文，第4段落第2文，最終段落第2文など，「人々が断食をする」との内容の英文がいずれも現在形で書かれているので，現在でも断食が行われていることがわかる。

⑦ 「医学的な問題に苦しんでいる患者を除けば，断食は危険である」

▶ 最終段落第1文に断食が危険であるとの記述があるが，例外については特に書かれていない。

それでは次に，段落ごとに詳しくみていこう。 🔊 07

第1段落　文の構造と語句のチェック

¹Why would someone decide to stop eating? ²We know 〈 that the body needs
food (in order to function well)〉. ³However, many people fast (at some time)
(during their lives). ⁴Why is this?

訳 ¹なぜ人は食べるのをやめようと決意するのだろうか。²身体は正しく機能するために食べ物を必要としていることを私たちは知っている。³しかし，多くの人々は人生の何らかの時に断食を行う。⁴これはなぜだろうか。

語句

in order to *do* 〔熟〕 ～するために
function 〔動〕 機能する

however 〔副〕 しかし
fast 〔動〕 断食する 〔名〕 断食

第2段落　文の構造と語句のチェック

¹Some people fast (for political reasons). ²(In the early 20th century),
women 〔 in England and the United States 〕 weren't allowed to vote. ³(In
protest), many women went on fasts. ⁴They hoped 〈 that fasting would bring
attention (to this injustice)〉. ⁵Mohandas Gandhi, the famous Indian leader,
fasted (17 times) (during his life). ⁶(For Gandhi), fasting was a powerful

32

political tool. ⁷(In 1943), he fasted (to bring attention (to his country's need
    C   S   V   V′   O′

[for independence])). ⁸(For 21 days), he went without food. ⁹Another famous
                                   S   V   O   S

faster was Cesar Chavez. ¹⁰(In the 1960s), he fasted (for three weeks).
  V   C   S   V

¹¹Why? ¹²His goal was ⟨ to bring attention (to the terrible working conditions
           S   V C V′   O′

[of farm workers in the United States])⟩.

訳 ¹政治的な理由で断食をする人々もいる。²20世紀初頭，イギリスやアメリカの女性たちは投票が許されていなかった。³それに抗議して，多くの女性達が断食を行った。⁴彼女たちは断食がこのような不公平への注意を喚起することを望んでいた。⁵インドの有名な指導者であるモーハンダース・ガンジーは，生涯に17回の断食を行った。⁶ガンジーにとっては，断食は強力な政治的手段だったのだ。⁷1943年に彼は，母国の独立の必要性に注意を喚起するために断食をした。⁸21日間，彼は食料なしで過ごしたのだ。⁹もう1人，断食をした有名人にセザール・チャベスがいる。¹⁰1960年代に彼は3週間の断食をした。¹¹なぜか。¹²彼の目標はアメリカの農場労働者達のひどい労働条件に注意を喚起することであった。

語句

political	形	政治的な	injustice	名 不公平，不公正
century	名	世紀	famous	形 有名な
allow	動	許可する	leader	名 指導者
vote	動	投票する	powerful	形 強力な
protest	名	抗議	tool	名 道具，手段
▶in protest	熟	抗議して	independence	名 独立
go on a fast	熟	断食する	go without ~	熟 ~なしで済ます
attention	名	注意，注目	faster	名 断食する人
▶bring attention to ~			goal	名 目標，目的
	熟	~への注意を喚起する	terrible	形 ひどい，ひどく悪い
			condition	名 条件，状況

¹Fasting is also a spiritual practice (in many religions). ²(Every year)
　　S　　V　　　　C

(during the month of Ramadan), which is a religious holiday, Muslims fast
　　　　　　　　　　　　　　　　関代　V　　　　C　　　　　　S　　V

(from sunrise to sunset). ³Many Hindus fast (on special occasions), (as do
　　　　　　　　　　　　　　　　　　S　　V　　　　　　　　　　　　　　従接　V

　①　　　　　等接　②
some Christians and Buddhists).
　　　　　S

> **訳** ¹断食はまた，多くの宗教における精神修行でもある。²毎年，宗教上の祭日であるラマ
> ダン月の間，イスラム教徒は日の出から日没まで断食をする。³多くのヒンドゥー教徒は，
> 一部のキリスト教徒や仏教徒と同様，特別な時に断食をする。

Check! 第3文 Many Hindus fast on special occasions, as do some Christians and Buddhists. の do は，前出の fast on special occasions の代用。as は【様態】の接続詞で，as の後では倒置が起こることがある。ここでは，do(=V) some Christians and Buddhists(=S)と倒置が起こっている。

語句

spiritual	形 精神的な	religious	形 宗教的な
practice	名 訓練，練習	sunrise	名 日の出
religion	名 宗教	sunset	名 日没
		occasion	名 時，場合

¹(Of course), not everyone fasts (for political or religious reasons).
　　　　　　　　　　　S　　　V　　　　　①　　　等接　②

²Some people occasionally fast (just because it makes them feel better). ³The
　　　S　　　　　　　V　　　　　　従接　S　V　O　　C

　　　　　　　　　　　　　　　　従接 that 省略
American writer Mark Twain thought 〔 fasting was the best medicine 〔 for
　　　　　同格　　　　　　　V　　　O　　　S　　V　　　C

common illnesses]〉. ⁴(Whenever he had a cold or a fever), he stopped eating
               従接   S   V   ①a cold 等接②or a fever   S   V   O

completely. ⁵He said 〈 that this always made his cold or fever go away 〉.
            S   V   O 従接 S   V   ①his cold 等接②or fever   C

⁶Another American writer, Upton Sinclair, discovered fasting (after years of
         S   └─同格─┘   V   O

overeating, stomach problems, and headaches). ⁷His first fast lasted (for 12
   ①   ②   等接   ③   S   V

days). ⁸(During this time), his headaches and stomachaches went away.
                        ①his headaches 等接②and stomachaches   V

⁹Sinclair said 〈 that fasting also made him more alert and energetic 〉.
 S   V   O従接 S   V   O   ①more alert   C ②and energetic 等接

> **訳** ¹もちろん，誰もが政治的あるいは宗教的な理由で断食をするわけではない。²単に気分を良くしてくれるからという理由で時々断食をする人もいる。³アメリカ人作家であるマーク・トウェインは，断食がよくある病気に対する最良の薬であると考えた。⁴彼は風邪を引いたり発熱したりするたびに，完全に食べることをやめた。⁵いつもこれによって風邪や発熱が治るのだと彼は言った。⁶また別のアメリカ人作家，アプトン・シンクレアは，長年にわたる過食，胃の不調，そして頭痛の末に断食を知った。⁷彼の初めての断食は12日間続いた。⁸この間に彼の頭痛や胃痛は治った。⁹シンクレアは，断食によってさらに頭の回転が速くなり精力的にもなったと言った。

🖊 **Check!** 第1文 Of course, not everyone fasts for political or religious reasons. の not everyone は，「誰もが〜というわけではない」の意味で**【部分否定】**を表す。

🖊 **Check!** 第2文 Some people occasionally fast just because it makes them feel better. の just because ... は「単に…というだけの理由で」の意味。simply because ... や merely because ... も同様の意味。

語句

of course	熟	もちろん
occasionally	副	時々，時たま
writer	名	作家
medicine	名	薬
common	形	一般的な，普通の
illness	名	病気
whenever	接	～するときはいつでも，～するたびに
cold	名	風邪
fever	名	熱，発熱
completely	副	完全に
go away	熟	消える，（病気が）治る
discover	動	発見する，気づく
overeating	名	過食
stomach	名	胃
headache	名	頭痛
stomachache	名	胃痛
last	動	続く，持続する
alert	形	機敏な，頭の回転が速い
energetic	形	精力的な

第5段落　文の構造と語句のチェック

¹Choosing to go without food can be very dangerous. ²However, that doesn't
 　　　　S　　　　　　　　　　　V　　　C　　　　　　　　　S　　V

stop people (from fasting (for political, religious, or health reasons)).
 O　　　　　　　①　　　　　②　　　等接　③

訳 ¹食べ物なしで済ますという選択は非常に危険な場合もある。²しかし，それでも人々は政治的，宗教的，あるいは健康上の理由から断食をすることをやめない。

語句

choose	動	選択する
stop O from *doing*	熟	O が～するのをやめさせる，O に～させない

文法事項の整理 ③　部分否定

第4段落第1文の not everyone についてみてみよう。

Of course, **not everyone** fasts for political or religious reasons.

「全部が～というわけではない，いつも～というわけではない」といった，「例外を認める否定」を【部分否定】という。

■部分否定の形

（1）副詞による部分否定

not ＋ always	「いつも〔必ずしも〕～というわけではない」
not ＋ necessarily	「必ずしも～というわけではない」
not ＋ everywhere	「どこでも～というわけではない」
not ＋ quite / altogether / completely / entirely / wholly	「まったく〔完全に〕～というわけではない」
not ＋ very / much / so / too	「あまり〔それほど / たいして〕～というわけではない」

（2）代名詞・形容詞の働きをする部分否定と全体否定

	2者	3者以上
部分否定	・not＋both（形 代） 「両方～というわけではない」	・not＋all（形 代） ・not＋every（形） 　「全て～というわけではない」
全体否定	・not＋either（形 代） 　*either＋not は× ・neither（形 代） 　「どちらも～ない」	・not＋any（形 代） 　*any＋not は× ・no（形） ・none（代） 　「まったく〔1つも〕～ない」

※形：形容詞の働きをし，直後に名詞がつく。
　代：代名詞の働きをし，単独でSやOになる。

（第4段落第1文）

Of course, not everyone fasts for political or religious reasons.

▶ 〈not＋every-〉なので，3者以上についての部分否定。

語句リストの復習

次の語句の意味を**ア～ト**からそれぞれ1つ選べ。

1 political	11 common	ア 熱	サ 完全に
2 religion	12 fever	イ 政治的な	シ 許可する
3 allow	13 discover	ウ 不公平	ス 独立
4 independence	14 choose	エ 目標	セ 条件，状況
5 vote	15 spiritual	オ 発見する	ソ 精神的な
6 goal	16 injustice	カ 薬	タ 宗教
7 protest	17 condition	キ 投票する	チ 胃
8 stomach	18 energetic	ク 精力的な	ツ 一般的な
9 occasionally	19 completely	ケ 時々	テ 抗議
10 medicine	20 function	コ 機能する	ト 選ぶ

答 1－イ　2－タ　3－シ　4－ス　5－キ　6－エ　7－テ　8－チ　9－ケ　10－カ
11－ツ　12－ア　13－オ　14－ト　15－ソ　16－ウ　17－セ　18－ク　19－サ　20－コ

ディクテーションしてみよう！　🔊 08-12

今回学習した英文に出てきた単語を，音声を聞いて（　　　）に書き取ろう。

Why would someone decide to stop eating? We know that the body needs food in order to ❶(f　　　　　　　) well. However, many people fast at some time during their lives. Why is this?

Some people fast for ❷(p　　　　　　) reasons. In the early 20th century, women in England and the United States weren't allowed to vote. In ❸(p　　　　), many women went on fasts. They hoped that fasting would bring attention to this injustice. Mohandas Gandhi, the famous Indian leader, fasted 17 times during his life. For Gandhi, fasting was a powerful political tool. In 1943, he fasted to bring attention to his country's need for

38

④(i   ). For 21 days, he went without food.
Another famous faster was Cesar Chavez. In the 1960s, he fasted
for three weeks. Why? His goal was to bring attention to the
terrible working **⑤**(c   ) of farm workers in the
United States.

Fasting is also a spiritual practice in many **⑥**(r   ).
Every year during the month of Ramadan, which is a religious
holiday, Muslims fast from sunrise to sunset. Many Hindus fast on
special occasions, as do some Christians and Buddhists.

Of course, not everyone fasts for political or religious reasons.
Some people **⑦**(o   ) fast just because it makes
them feel better. The American writer Mark Twain thought fasting
was the best medicine for **⑧**(c   ) illnesses. Whenever he
had a cold or a fever, he stopped eating completely. He said that this
always made his cold or **⑨**(f   ) go away. Another American
writer, Upton Sinclair, discovered fasting after years of overeating,
⑩(s   ) problems, and headaches. His first fast lasted for
12 days. During this time, his headaches and stomachaches went
away. Sinclair said that fasting also made him more alert and
energetic.

⑪(C   ) to go without food can be very dangerous.
However, that doesn't stop people from fasting for political, religious,
or health reasons.

答 **❶** function　　**❷** political　　**❸** protest　　**❹** independence　　**❺** conditions　　**❻** religions
　　❼ occasionally　　**❽** common　　**❾** fever　　**❿** stomach　　**⓫** Choosing

解 答

問1	②，④，⑤，⑦，⑧
問2	**（ウ）** the United Nations ［または the International Committee for the Red Cross］
	（エ） the International Committee for the Red Cross
問3	受賞者が資金調達の心配をしなくても仕事や研究を継続できるようにすること。
問4	**（ア）** アルフレッド・ノーベルは，ダイナマイトという強力な爆発物を発明した人物であった。
	（イ） 後に，1968 年に，スウェーデン銀行が同行の創業 300 周年を記念して経済学の分野での賞を加えた。

解 説

問1

① 「ノーベル賞はアルフレッド・ノーベルとともに働いた世界中の人々に与えられる」

▶ ノーベル賞受賞者の条件は第1段落第2文，第2段落第2文に記述があるが，「ノーベルとともに働いた」との内容は含まれていない。

② 「アルフレッド・ノーベルは発明家で，ノーベル賞を設立した」

▶ 第1段落第2文と一致。

③ 「1901 年に6つのノーベル賞が初めて授与された」

▶ 第3段落第1文より，1901 年には5部門のみ授与されたことがわかる。

④ 「経済学の分野での賞が後に加えられた」

▶ 第3段落第2文と一致。

⑤ 「ノーベル賞受賞者は現金を含む3つのものを与えられる」

▶ 第4段落第1文と一致。

⑥「金大中，大江健三郎，ネルソン・マンデラは皆，平和賞の受賞者である」

▶ 第5段落第2文により，大江健三郎は文学賞の受賞者とわかる。

⑦「**赤十字国際委員会はジャン・アンリ・デュナンによって創立された**」

▶ 最終段落第2文後半と一致。

⑧「**ジャン・アンリ・デュナンは1901年の最初のノーベル賞受賞者の1人であった**」

▶ 最終段落第2文後半と一致。

問2

（ウ） ノーベル賞受賞者の団体は，第5段落第2文の the United Nations と，第6段落第1文の the International Committee for the Red Cross の2つが挙げられている。

（エ） this は原則として直前の文に指示内容がある。

問3

　第4段落第2文後半参照。aim は「目的，目標」の意味で，具体的な内容が to 以下に書かれている。

問4

（ア） 以下のポイントをおさえよう！

☑ who は関係代名詞で，先行詞は the man。

☑ dynamite の後の「コンマ(,)」は【同格】を表す。〈名詞 A，名詞 B〉で A と B が同格となる場合，「**A つまり B，A という B，A である B**」（それぞれ A と B を逆にしても可）などの訳が可能。

（イ） 以下のポイントをおさえよう！

☑ the Bank of Sweden が S，added が V，a prize in economics が O。

☑ to celebrate 以下は不定詞の副詞用法で【目的】を表す。

☑ celebrate は「〜を祝う，記念する」。

☑ the bank's 300th year of business は直訳すれば「その銀行の営業の300年目」。「同行の創業300周年」など自然な日本語にするとよい。

なお，Later をより具体的に言い換えたのが，コンマの後ろの in 1968 である。

第1段落　文の構造と語句のチェック

¹(Each year)(on December 10), <u>the world's attention</u> <u>turns</u> (to Sweden)
　　　　　　　　　　　　　　　　　S　　　　　　　　　V

(for the announcement 〔 of the Nobel Prize winners 〕). ²<u>The Nobel Prizes, six</u>
　　　　　　　　　　　　　　　　　　　　　　　　　　　　　S　　　　└同格─

<u>prizes</u> 〔 given to groups or individuals 〔 who really <u>stand out</u> (in their fields)〕〕,
　　　　　　　　　　　①　等接　　②　　　関代　　　　V

<u>were founded</u> (by a Swedish inventor, Alfred Nobel).
　　V　　　　　　　　　　　　　└同格─

> **訳** ¹毎年 12 月 10 日，世界の注目はノーベル賞受賞者の発表のためスウェーデンに向けられる。²ノーベル賞は，各自の分野で本当に際立った集団または個人に与えられる 6 つの賞で，スウェーデンの発明家であるアルフレッド・ノーベルによって創立された。

Check! 第 2 文 The Nobel Prizes, six prizes given to groups or individuals who really stand out in their fields, were founded by a Swedish inventor, Alfred Nobel. の The Nobel Prizes と six prizes … fields，そして a Swedish inventor と Alfred Nobel が，それぞれ【同格】になっている。〈名詞 A，名詞 B〉で，A と B のいずれかを取り除いても文が成立する場合，A と B が同格〔言い換え〕となっている場合が多い。

語句

each year	熟	毎年
attention	名	注意，注目
turn to ~	熟	~に向く
announcement	名	発表
prize	名	賞

winner	名	受賞者
individual	名	個人
stand out	熟	目立つ，注目を浴びる
field	名	分野
found	動	創立する，設立する
inventor	名	発明家

第2段落 文の構造と語句のチェック

[1]Alfred Nobel was the man 〔 who invented dynamite, a powerful explosive 〕.
S　　　　　V　　C　　　関代　　V　　　　　O └─同格─┘

[2](During his life), Nobel made a lot of money (from his invention), and he
S　　V　　O　　　　　　　　　　　　　　等接　S

decided 〈 that he wanted to use his money (to help scientists, artists, and
V　　O 従接 S　　V　　　O　　　V'　　　O'　　等接

people 〔 who worked (to help others around the world)〕〉. [3](When he died),
関代　V　　　　　　　　　　　　　　　　　　　　従接 S　V

his will said 〈 that the money would be placed (in a bank), and the interest
S　　V　O 従接　S　　　V　　　　　　　　　　　等接　S
┌─── 関代 which の省略
〔the money earned 〕 would be given out (as five annual cash prizes)〉.
S'　　V'　　　　V

> 訳 [1]アルフレッド・ノーベルは，ダイナマイトという強力な爆発物を発明した人物である。
> [2]生涯の間に，ノーベルは発明により多くの金を稼いだ。そして，自分の金を，科学者や芸
> 術家，そして世界中の他者を助けるために働いている人々を援助するために使いたいと心
> に決めた。[3]彼が死んだとき，彼の遺言には，その金は銀行に預け，その金で得た利子は毎
> 年5つの賞金として分配するものとする，とあった。

Check! 第3文 … and the interest the money earned would be given out as five
annual cash prizes. の interest の後に，関係代名詞 that [which] が省略されて
いる。

語句

invent	動	発明する
dynamite	名	ダイナマイト
powerful	形	強力な
explosive	名	爆発物
invention	名	発明
will	名	遺書，遺言

place	動	預ける
interest	名	利子，利息
earn	動	稼ぐ，（利子が）つく
give out ~	熟	～を分配する
annual	形	毎年の
cash	名	現金
▶ cash prize	名	賞金

[1]The prizes 〔 set up by Nobel 〕 were first handed out (in 1901), and included
S / V① / 等接 / V②

①physics, ②medicine, ③chemistry, ④literature, and ⑤peace. [2](Later), (in 1968) the
O / 等接

Bank of Sweden added a prize in economics (to celebrate the bank's 300th year
S / V / O / V' / O'

of business).

> **訳** [1]ノーベルによって創設された賞は 1901 年に初めて授与され，物理学，医学，化学，文学，平和の各賞が含まれていた。[2]後に，1968 年に，スウェーデン銀行が創業 300 周年を記念して経済学の分野での賞を加えた。

語句

set up ~	熟	～を創設する，設ける
hand out ~	熟	～を配る，～を手渡す
include	動	含む
physics	名	物理学
medicine	名	医学
chemistry	名	化学

literature	名	文学
peace	名	平和
later	副	後に
add	動	加える
economics	名	経済学
celebrate	動	祝う，記念する
business	名	事業，営業

[1]Each person 〔 who receives a Nobel Prize 〕 is given ①a cash prize, ②a medal, and
S / 関代 / V / O / V / O / 等接

③a certificate. [2]The prize money 〔 for each category 〕 is currently worth
S / V

about a million dollars, and the aim of the prize is ⟨ to allow the winner to carry
C / 等接 / S / V / C / V' / O'

①on working or ②researching (without having to worry (about raising money))⟩.
C' / 等接

44

訳 ¹ノーベル賞の各受賞者は賞金とメダルと証明書を授与される。²各部門の賞金は現在のところ，およそ100万ドル相当となっており，賞の目的は，受賞者が資金調達の心配なく仕事や研究を続けられるようにすることである。

Check! 第2文の worth は前置詞（形容詞という考え方もある）で「〜の価値がある，〜に値する」。

例 This watch is worth 1,000 dollars.
「この時計は1000ドルの価値がある」

Check! 第2文の allow O to *do* は「Oが〜することを許可する」のほか，「Oが〜することを可能にする」の意味もある。

第2文の without having to worry … は，without *doing*「〜せずに」と have to *do*「〜しなければならない」が組み合わさった表現。

語句

receive	動 受け取る	worth	前 〜の価値がある
medal	名 メダル，勲章	aim	名 目的，目標
certificate	名 証明書	allow	動 可能にする
category	名 部門，区分	carry on doing	熟 〜し続ける
currently	副 現在のところ	raise	動 (金を)集める，調達する

第5段落 文の構造と語句のチェック

¹The prizes can be given (to either individuals or groups). ²Prize winners include Albert Einstein (physics, 1921), Kenzaburo Oe (literature, 1994), Kim Dae Jung (peace, 2001), the United Nations (peace, 2001), and Nelson Mandela (peace, 1993).

訳 [1]ノーベル賞は個人または団体のいずれかに授与されうる。[2]受賞者にはアルバート・アインシュタイン（物理学賞，1921年），大江健三郎（文学賞，1994年），金大中（平和賞，2001年），国際連合（平和賞，2001年），そしてネルソン・マンデラ（平和賞，1993年）が含まれる。

語句

either *A* or *B* 熟 AかBのいずれか

第6段落　文の構造と語句のチェック

[1]The prize winner [that has won (the most times)] is the International
　　　　 S 　　　　　 関代　 V 　　　　　　　　　　　　　 V

Committee for the Red Cross. [2]This organization has received three Nobel
　　　　　 C 　　　　　　　　　　　　 S 　　　　　 V

Peace Prizes (in 1917, 1944, and 1963), and the founder, Jean Henri Dunant,
　　 O 　　　　　　　　　　　　　　　　 等接　 S 　└─同格─┘

was awarded the first Nobel Peace Prize, (in 1901).
　 V 　　　　　 O

訳 [1]もっとも受賞回数の多い受賞者は，赤十字国際委員会である。[2]この団体はノーベル平和賞を3回(1917年，1944年，1963年)受賞し，創立者であるジャン・アンリ・デュナンは初めてのノーベル平和賞を1901年に授与された。

語句

committee 名 委員会
organization 名 組織，団体

founder 名 創立者
award 動 (賞を)与える，授与する

文法事項の整理 ④ 挿入句

第1段落第2文の挿入句についてみてみよう。

The Nobel Prizes, six prizes given to groups of individuals who really stand out in their fields, were founded by ...

コンマ(,)で挟まれていて，その部分をとばして読んでも，前後がつながるような場合，コンマに挟まれている句を【挿入句】と言う。

挿入句にはいくつかの働きがあるので，整理しよう。

■挿入句の種類

(1) 直前部分と同格(言い換え)

▶「つまり」「すなわち」「という」「である」などと訳す。

例　Tokyo, the capital of Japan, is an exciting city.

「東京，つまり日本の首都は〔日本の首都である東京は〕，わくわくする都市である」

(2) 主節にあたるものの挿入

▶最初か最後に訳す。

例　Your plan is, everybody will agree, not easy to carry out.

「みんな意見が一致するだろうが，君の計画は実行するのが容易ではない」

(= Everybody will agree (that) your plan is not easy to carry out.)

(3) 副詞(句・節)の挿入

▶語順どおりに訳してもよいし，最初に訳してもよい。

例　You should, if possible, go to the dentist.

「君は，可能なら歯医者に行くべきだ〔可能なら，君は歯医者に行くべきだ〕」

※ただし，直前の文との論理関係を示す副詞が挿入されている場合，必ず最初に訳す。

例　He isn't a hardworking student.　In the exams, however, he always gets a high score.

「彼は勤勉な学生ではない。しかし，試験ではいつも高得点を取る」

（第1段落第2文）

The Nobel Prizes, <u>six prizes given to groups or individuals who really stand out in their fields</u>, were founded by ...

▶(1)の同格の用法。

（第6段落第2文）

... and the founder, <u>Jean Henri Dunant</u>, was awarded the first Nobel Peace Prize, in 1901.

▶(1)の同格の用法。

語句リストの復習

次の語句の意味を**ア〜ト**からそれぞれ1つ選べ。

/20点

1	announcement	11	receive
2	chemistry	12	certificate
3	prize	13	raise
4	will	14	award
5	individual	15	medicine
6	interest	16	found
7	stand out	17	physics
8	committee	18	organization
9	literature	19	aim
10	celebrate	20	attention

ア	化学	サ	創立する
イ	注意	シ	目的
ウ	（賞を）与える	ス	受け取る
エ	（金を）集める	セ	遺書
オ	祝う	ソ	発表
カ	委員会	タ	組織
キ	目立つ	チ	利子
ク	個人	ツ	医学
ケ	賞	テ	証明書
コ	文学	ト	物理学

答 1−ソ　2−ア　3−ケ　4−セ　5−ク　6−チ　7−キ　8−カ　9−コ　10−オ
11−ス　12−テ　13−エ　14−ウ　15−ツ　16−サ　17−ト　18−タ　19−シ　20−イ

ディクテーションしてみよう！　🔊 14-19

今回学習した英文に出てきた単語を，音声を聞いて（　　　）に書き取ろう。

Each year on December 10, the world's **❶**(a　　　　　) turns to Sweden for the announcement of the Nobel Prize winners. The Nobel Prizes, six prizes given to groups or individuals who really **❷**(s　　) out in their fields, were **❸**(f　　　) by a Swedish inventor, Alfred Nobel.

Alfred Nobel was the man who invented dynamite, a powerful explosive. During his life, Nobel made a lot of money from his invention, and he decided that he wanted to use his money to help scientists, artists, and people who worked to help others around the world. When he died, his **❹**(w　　) said that the money would be placed in a bank, and the **❺**(i　　　　) the money earned would be given out as five annual cash prizes.

The prizes set up by Nobel were first handed out in 1901, and included physics, **❻**(m　　　　　), chemistry, literature, and peace. Later, in 1968 the Bank of Sweden added a prize in economics to **❼**(c　　　　) the bank's 300th year of business.

Each person who **❽**(r　　　) a Nobel Prize is given a cash prize, a medal, and a certificate. The prize money for each category is currently worth about a million dollars, and the **❾**(a　) of the prize is to allow the winner to carry on working or researching without having to worry about **❿**(r　　　　) money.

The prizes can be given to either **⓫**(i　　　　) or groups. Prize winners include Albert Einstein (physics, 1921), Kenzaburo Oe (literature, 1994), Kim Dae Jung (peace, 2001), the United Nations (peace, 2001), and Nelson Mandela (peace, 1993).

The prize winner that has won the most times is the International Committee for the Red Cross. This organization has received three Nobel Peace Prizes (in 1917, 1944, and 1963), and the founder, Jean Henri Dunant, was awarded the first Nobel Peace Prize, in 1901.

答 **❶** attention　**❷** stand　**❸** founded　**❹** will　**❺** interest　**❻** medicine　**❼** celebrate　**❽** receives　**❾** aim　**❿** raising　**⓫** individuals

5 解答・解説

解答

問1	③	問2	③	問3	②	問4	④	問5	③
問6	④	問7	②	問8	④	問9	①	問10	③

解説

問1 「多くの人々が知らないことは何か」

① 「小さな成功は失敗と異なることが多い」

② 「失敗と成功は異なることが多い」

③ **「成功と失敗の間には小さな違いがあることが多い」**

④ 「失敗とは小さな成功であることが多い」

▶ 第1段落第1文参照。

問2 「金メダルを獲得する人物は＿＿＿＿＿＿人であることが多い」

① 「10倍速い」

② 「2倍速い」

③ **「少しだけ速い」**

④ 「決してあきらめない」

▶ 第3段落第4，5文参照。

問3 「『小さな違いが大きな違いを作り出すかもしれない』は＿＿＿＿＿＿と
いうことを意味する」

① 「成功はちょっとした運によることが多い」

② **「成功は小さな事柄によることが多い」**

③ 「決してあきらめてはならない」

④ 「人生はしばしば真実だ」

▶ 設問文中の引用部分は第1段落第4文。この前後の内容から考える。本文で
は「運」については言及されていないことに注意。

問4 「勝者と敗者の違いは＿＿＿＿＿＿ことが多い」

① 「かなり大きい」

② 「大きい」

③「2倍優れている」

④「たいしたことはない」

▶ 第1段落第3文, 第3段落第3文参照。なお, ① quite a bit は「相当な, かなりの」(≒quite a little)の意味である点にも注意。

問5 「本文によれば, _____ はたいていの場合, 成功につながる」

①「わずかな時だけ, 大部分が優れていること」

②「ほとんどの時に, はるかに優れていること」

③**「1, 2パーセントを反復すること」**

④「将来において完璧となること」

▶ 第4段落第1文参照。

問6 「本文によれば, 私たちはもし_____ならばもっと成功できる」

①「私たちが天才である」

②「私たちが10倍優れている」

③「私たちが完璧である」

④**「私たちが少しだけ優れている」**

▶ 第4段落全体, および最終段落第4文参照。

問7 「英雄は_____」

①「とてつもない力を持っている」

②**「たいてい少しだけ優れているので, 成功する」**

③「他者とは大きく異なる」

④「平均よりもさほど美しくない」

▶ 最終段落第1〜3文参照。

問8 「第1段落の最後の部分で, "the small difference is regular and repeated" という表現は_____を意味している」

①「何度も繰り返し練習すること」

②「小さな違いとはわずか1, 2パーセントでしかないことが多いこと」

③「小さな違い」

④**「一連の小さな違い」**

▶ 引用部分は「小さな違いが定期的で繰り返される」という意味。この後の第2段落の具体例も参考になる。

問9 「本文の最後の "result" は_____のことを言っている」

① 「あなたの成功」

② 「あなたの努力」

③ 「より熱心に努力すること」

④ 「ちょっとした失敗」

▶ 最終段落後半は小さな努力の積み重ねが成功につながるとの内容。したがって「結果」とは「成功」のことである。

問10 「本文にもっともふさわしいタイトルはどれか」

① 「習うより慣れろ」

② 「小さな成功」

③ 「成功する方法」

④ 「違いを生じない方法」

▶ 本文では成功と失敗の差はわずかであることを具体例を挙げて示した上で，最終段落であともう少しの努力をすることを勧めている。そのことが成功につながるのだとしている。よって③が正解。①の Practice makes perfect. は「練習が完璧を作り上げる」→「習うより慣れろ」という意味のことわざ。

▼

それでは次に，段落ごとに詳しくみていこう。　🔊 **20**

第1段落　文の構造と語句のチェック

¹Many people don't know 〈 that the difference 〔 between success and failure 〕
S　　　　　　V　　　O　従接　　　　S

is often very small 〉. ²One does not need to be twice as good, (let alone perfect),
V　　　C　　　　S　　　　　V　　　　　C

(in order to succeed (in most things)). ³(In fact), often only a tiny difference
S

separates winners and losers. ⁴A small difference may make a big difference.
V　　　O　　　　O　　　　S　　　　　V　　　　O

52

⁵This is true (in many areas of life), (especially if the small difference is
　S　V　C　　　　　　　　　　　　　　　　　　　　従接　　　S　　　　　V
①　　　等接 ②
regular and repeated).
　　　　　　C

訳 ¹多くの人々は，成功と失敗の違いがごく小さいものである場合が多いということを知らない。²ほとんどの物事において成功するためには，（他者より）2倍も優れている必要はなく，まして完璧である必要はないのだ。³実際は，ほんのちっぽけな差が勝者と敗者を分ける場合が多い。⁴小さな違いが大きな違いを作り出すかもしれないのだ。⁵このことは人生の多くの面において，特に小さな違いが定期的で反復される場合に当てはまる。

Check! 第2文 One does not need to be twice as good, let alone perfect, in order to succeed in most things. の主語 One は「一般の人」を表しており，通常は訳さない。

語句

difference	名	違い	tiny	形	とても小さい，ごくわずかの
success	名	成功	separate	動	分ける，（勝敗を）決める
failure	名	失敗	winner	名	勝者
let alone ~	熟	まして~はなおさら	loser	名	敗者
in order to *do*	熟	~するために	area	名	領域，分野
succeed	動	成功する	especially	副	特に
in fact	熟	実際に	regular	形	定期的な，いつもの
			repeat	動	反復する

第2段落　文の構造と語句のチェック

¹(For example), consider two clocks, [running at a speed [differing only by
　　　　　　　　　　　V　　　　O
one second per hour]]. ²Only one second per hour doesn't seem like much, but
　　　　　　　　　　　　　S　　　　　　　　　　　　　　V　　　　C　　　等接
it is almost a half minute per day, or almost three minutes a week, or
S　V　　　　　　　　　　　C①　　　等接　　　　　　　　　C②　　　　　　　等接

about twelve minutes a month, and almost two and a half hours a year. ³Well,
　　　　　　　　C③　　　　　等接　　　　　　　　　　　　　　C④

there's actually quite a difference (between those two clocks).
　　 V　　　　　　 S

訳 ¹たとえば，1 時間につき 1 秒だけ異なるスピードで進む 2 つの時計を考えてみなさい。
²1 時間につきたった 1 秒はたいしたことがないように思われるが，1 日あたりほぼ 30 秒
であり，1 週間あたりほぼ 3 分であり，1 カ月あたりほぼ 12 分であり，1 年あたりだと
ほぼ 2 時間半である。³そう，これらの 2 つの時計の間には実際にはかなりの違いが存在
するのだ。

語句

for example	熟	たとえば	per	前 ～につき，～ごとに
consider	動	考える，検討する	almost	副 ほぼ，ほとんど
differ	動	異なる	actually	副 実際は
second	名	秒	quite	副 かなり，なかなか
			▶ quite a ～	熟 かなりの～

第 3 段落　文の構造と語句のチェック

¹Sports is another good example. ²One doesn't have to be much better (than
　S　　V　　　　　C　　　　　　 S　　　　　 V　　　　　　C

others) (to win). ³The difference 〔 between winning and losing 〕 is often
　　　　　　　　　　　 S　　　　　　　　　　　　　　　　　　　　V

very small. ⁴(At the Olympics), the difference 〔 between winning and losing 〕
　 C　　　　　　　　　　　　　　　　　　　 S

is often just 0.1 second or just a centimeter or two. ⁵Such a small difference
 V　　　　　　 C①　　 等接　　　 C②　　　　　　　　　　　　 S

can determine 〈 who gets a gold medal 〉.
　　 V　　　 O 疑　 V　　 O

訳 ¹スポーツはもう 1 つの好例だ。²勝つためには他者よりもずっと優れている必要はない。
³勝つか負けるかの違いは非常に些細なものであることが多い。⁴オリンピックでは，勝敗
の違いはわずか 0.1 秒あるいは 1，2 センチであることがよくある。⁵そのようなちょっと
した差が，誰が金メダルを獲得するかを決定することがあり得るのだ。

Check! 第5文 Such a small difference can determine who gets a gold medal. の who は，関係代名詞ではなく疑問詞。「誰が〜か」の意味で，名詞節を導く。ここでは who の導く節が determine の目的語になっている。

語句

another	形	他の，もう1つの
example	名	例
second	名	秒
centimeter	名	センチメートル
determine	動	決定する，左右する
medal	名	メダル

第4段落　文の構造と語句のチェック

¹A small difference, often just a percent or two, (if repeated over and over),
（従接）／it is 省略

will almost always lead to success [in the future]. ²One does not need to be
a genius, does not need to be ten times better, or even twice as good, (let alone
perfect). ³Just a small difference is usually enough (to succeed).

訳 ¹ちょっとした違い，しばしばたった1，2パーセントの違いが何度も反復されると，ほぼ確実に将来における成功につながるのだ。²天才である必要はなく，10倍も優れている必要はなく，2倍優れている必要さえなく，まして完璧である必要はない。³ほんのわずかの違いが，たいていの場合，成功には十分なのだ。

語句

percent	名	パーセント
over and over	熟	何度も繰り返し
lead to 〜	熟	〜につながる，〜を引き起こす
future	名	未来，将来
genius	名	天才

¹Our heroes seem to have superpowers, but actually they are just normal
 S   V   O   等接   S   V

people. ²They are not really that much different (from us). ³They are just a
  C   S   V   C   S   V

tiny bit faster, or smarter, or more beautiful (than average). ⁴(If one wants to
   C①   等接   C②   等接   C③   従接 S   V

be successful), just remember ⟨ that the difference 〔 between success and
   C   V   O 従接   S

failure 〕 is often very small ⟩. ⁵So why don't you try (just a little harder), (a
           V   C   等接   (V)   S   V

little more often)? ⁶A small difference may make a big difference. ⁷You may be
                        S   V   O   S   V

surprised (by the result).
    C

訳 ¹私たちの英雄はとてつもない力を持っているように思われるが，実際には単なる普通の人々なのだ。²彼らは本当は私たちと大して変わらないのである。³ただ，平均よりもちょっとだけ速かったり，頭が良かったり，美しかったりするだけなのだ。⁴もし成功したいのであれば，成功と失敗の違いは多くの場合，とてもわずかだということをとにかく忘れないようにしなさい。⁵だから，もう少しだけ一生懸命に，もう少しだけ頻繁に，努力してみてはどうだろうか。⁶わずかな違いが大きな違いを生じるかもしれない。⁷その結果に驚くかもしれない。

語句

hero	名 英雄	**smart**	形 利口な，頭の良い
superpower	名 非常に大きな力	average	名 平均
normal	形 普通の，標準の	successful	形 成功して
bit	名 ちょっと，少し	result	名 結果

文法事項の整理 ⑤　副詞節中の〈S＋be〉の省略

第4段落第1文の if repeated over and over についてみてみよう。

A small difference, often just a percent or two, **if repeated over and over**, will almost always lead to success in the future.

【時】【条件】【譲歩】の副詞節中の〈S＋be 動詞〉は，S が文全体の S と同じなら省略することができる。

＊【時】を表す副詞節：when ...,　while ...,
＊【条件】を表す副詞節：if ...,　unless ...,
＊【譲歩】を表す副詞節：though ...,　although ...,

■副詞節中の〈S＋be 動詞〉の省略

例　She fell asleep while she was watching television.　【時】の副詞節
　　「彼女はテレビを見ている間に眠ってしまった」

例　This machine will be of great use if it is properly used.　【条件】の副詞節
　　「この機械は適切に使えば非常に役立つ」

例　I didn't drink water though I was thirsty.　【譲歩】の副詞節
　　「私はのどが渇いていたが，水を飲まなかった」

副詞節中の S が文全体の S と同じでなくても，文脈上明らかな場合は省略されることがある。

例　I will finish this work by tomorrow if it is possible.
　　「可能ならば明日までにこの仕事を終えるつもりだ」

（第4段落第1文）

A small difference, often just a percent or two, <u>if repeated</u> over and over, will almost always lead to success in the future.

▶下線部は，if it is repeated の it is が省略されている（【条件】の副詞節）。

語句リストの復習

次の語句の意味を**ア〜ト**からそれぞれ１つ選べ。

/20点

1	success	11	determine
2	per	12	over and over
3	failure	13	normal
4	especially	14	result
5	let alone 〜	15	differ
6	regular	16	area
7	tiny	17	consider
8	smart	18	average
9	actually	19	genius
10	example	20	difference

ア	〜につき	サ	違い
イ	考える	シ	天才
ウ	利口な	ス	成功
エ	領域	セ	まして(〜ない)
オ	結果	ソ	とても小さい
カ	普通の	タ	特に
キ	何度も繰り返し	チ	定期的な
ク	失敗	ツ	異なる
ケ	平均	テ	実際は
コ	決定する	ト	例

答 1−ス 2−ア 3−ク 4−タ 5−セ 6−チ 7−ソ 8−ウ 9−テ 10−ト
11−コ 12−キ 13−カ 14−オ 15−ツ 16−エ 17−イ 18−ケ 19−シ 20−サ

ディクテーションしてみよう！ 🔊 21-25

今回学習した英文に出てきた単語を，音声を聞いて( )に書き取ろう。

Many people don't know that the difference between success and failure is often very small. One does not need to be twice as good, let ❶(a   ) perfect, in order to succeed in most things. In fact, often only a tiny difference separates winners and losers. A small difference may make a big difference. This is true in many ❷(a   ) of life, especially if the small difference is regular and repeated.

For example, ❸(c   ) two clocks, running at a speed differing only by one second per hour. Only one second per hour doesn't seem like much, but it is almost a half minute per day, or almost three minutes a week, or about twelve minutes a month, and almost two and a half hours a year. Well, there's ^❹(a   ) quite a difference between those two clocks.

Sports is another good ^❺(e   ). One doesn't have to be much better than others to win. The difference between winning and losing is often very small. At the Olympics, the difference between winning and losing is often just 0.1 second or just a centimeter or two. Such a small difference can ^❻(d   ) who gets a gold medal.

A small difference, often just a percent or two, if repeated over and over, will almost always lead to success in the future. One does not need to be a ^❼(g   ), does not need to be ten times better, or even twice as good, let alone perfect. Just a small difference is usually enough to succeed.

Our heroes seem to have superpowers, but actually they are just ^❽(n   ) people. They are not really that much different from us. They are just a tiny bit faster, or ^❾(s   ), or more beautiful than ^❿(a   ). If one wants to be successful, just remember that the difference between success and failure is often very small. So why don't you try just a little harder, a little more often? A small difference may make a big difference. You may be surprised by the ^⓫(r   ).

答 ❶ alone ❷ areas ❸ consider ❹ actually ❺ example ❻ determine ❼ genius ❽ normal ❾ smarter ❿ average ⓫ result

問 （ア）③ 　（イ）① 　（ウ）② 　（エ）③ 　（オ）④

解 説

問1

（ア）「ドリス・ヴァン・カッペルホフは_____」

① 「卒業式に向かう途中，自動車事故で負傷した」

② 「将来はハリウッド映画の中で演じたいと思っていた」

③ **「ハリウッド映画に出るダンサーになることをあきらめた」**

④ 「数年間入院していた」

▶ ③が第1段落第2文と一致。①に関しては，第1段落第1文に「卒業パーティーの日の夜に」とあるが，「卒業式に行く途中で」とは書かれていない。②は第1段落第2文の内容と似ているが，映画のダンサーになるためにハリウッドに行くことと，ハリウッド映画で役者として演技をすることの違いを考慮すると，③のほうが適切。④は第1段落第3文と不一致。

（イ）「ドリスは_____によって歌の技術を向上させた」

① **「ラジオの女性歌手と一緒に歌うこと」**

② 「ハリウッド映画の中で役を演じること」

③ 「プロのバンドで雇われて歌うこと」

④ 「本当の天職を見つけること」

▶ 第1段落第3，4文参照。選択肢②，③，④もそれぞれ近い記述はあるのだが，これらは歌の技術を向上させた手段ではなく，むしろその結果である。

（ウ）「筆者は私たちが_____と信じている」

① 「他人の行動のしかたをコントロールしようとしている」

② **「人生で何が起こるかを完全に知ることは決してできない」**

③ 「物事が自分の希望に反して起こることをめったに恐れない」

④ 「世の中が私たちに報いてくれると期待すべきだ」

▶ 第1段落最終文，最終段落第2文参照。

（エ）「ローバー・バーンズが言おうとしていることは_____ということである」

① 「私たちは最善の計画を立てれば生活を向上させることができる」

② 「私たちは不運だと哀れな生活を送らなければならないことが多い」

③ **「最善の計画でさえ悲しくて痛ましい結果になりかねない」**

④ 「最善の計画があれば私たちは落胆せずにすむだろう」

▶ 第3段落最終文参照。

(オ) 「この文章にもっとも適切なタイトルは＿＿＿＿である」

① 「人生は必ずしも公平ではない」

② 「他人の感情を受け止める方法」

③ 「人はどんなときでも愛情豊かで忠実でいられるわけではない」

④ **「物事は必ずしも計画通りに進行するわけではない」**

▶ ④の内容は第1段落最終文，第2段落最終文，第4段落第2文などに書かれている。

それでは次に，段落ごとに詳しくみていこう。　 26

第1段落　文の構造と語句のチェック

¹(In the early 1940s), (on the night of her graduation party), a high school
<u>　　　　　　　　　　　　　　　　　　　　　　　　　　　　　　　　　　　</u>
　　　　　　　　　　　　　　　　　　　　　　　　　　　　　　　　　　　S

girl 〔named Doris Van Kappelhoff 〕 <u>was</u> <u>involved</u> (in a serious car accident).
<u>　　</u>　　　　　　　　　　　　　　　V　　　C

²<u>She</u> <u>had planned to go</u> (to Hollywood) (to become a dancer in films), but
　S　　V　　　　　　　　　　　　　　　　　　　　　　　　　　　　　　　　　等接

<u>her injuries</u> <u>made</u> <u>that future</u> <u>no longer possible</u>. ³(During her long recovery 〔 at
　S　　　　　V　　　O　　　　　　C

home 〕), <u>Doris</u> <u>began to sing</u> (along with the female vocalists 〔 on the radio 〕).
　　　　　S　　V

⁴<u>Her voice</u> <u>became</u> so <u>well trained</u> that <u>she</u> <u>was hired</u> (to sing in a band), and
　S　　　　V　　　　　C　　　　　　S　　V　　　　　　　　　　　　　　　　　等接

(soon thereafter), <u>she</u> <u>found</u> <u>parts</u> 〔 in movies 〕, (<u>changing</u> <u>her name</u> to Doris
　　　　　　　　　　S　　V　　O　　　　　　　　　　V'　　　O'

Day). ⁵Her original plans were destroyed (by a tragic event), but thereby she
　　　　　　S　　　　　　　V　　　　　　　　　　　　　　　　等接　　　　　　S

found her true calling. ⁶Things don't always go (according to our plans), but
　V　　O　　　　　　　S　　　　V　　　　　　　　　　　　　　　　等接

a change of plans may be an example [of coincidental circumstances [that lead
　　　S　　　　　V　　C　　　　　　　　　　　　　　　　　　　　　関代　V

us (to a fulfilling life, [unguessed and unsought] — a blessing from God)]].
O　　　　　　　　　①　　　　　　　等接　②
　　　　　　　　　　　　　　　　　└─同格─┘

> **訳** ¹1940 年代はじめ，卒業パーティーの日の夜，ドリス・ヴァン・カッペルホフという
> 名前の女子高校生が重大な自動車事故に巻き込まれた。²彼女は映画に出るダンサーになる
> ためにハリウッドに行くことを計画していたのだが，負傷のせいで，もはやその将来の可
> 能性はなくなってしまった。³回復するまでの自宅での長い期間，ドリスはラジオの女性歌
> 手たちと一緒に歌い始めた。⁴彼女の声は非常に良く訓練されたものになったため，雇われ
> てバンドで歌うようになり，その後すぐに映画での配役をもらい，名前もドリス・デイに
> 改めた。⁵彼女の当初の計画は悲劇的な出来事によって打ち砕かれてしまったが，それによ
> って彼女は本当の天職を見出したのだ。⁶物事は必ずしも計画に従って進むわけではない
> が，計画の変更は，私たちを予想も期待もしていなかった充実した人生——神様からの恵
> み——に導いてくれるような偶然の出来事の一例となるかもしれないのだ。

Ⓒ 第 6 文 Things don't always go according to our plans, … の not always は
Check! 「必ずしも～ではない，いつも～とは限らない」の意味で，**【部分否定】**を表す。

語句

graduation	名	卒業		**hire**	動	雇う
be involved in ~	熟	~に巻き込まれている		band	名	バンド，楽団
serious	形	深刻な，重大な		thereafter	副	その後
plan to do	熟	~しようと計画する		part	名	(劇などの)役，配役
film	名	映画		**original**	形	最初の，本来の
injury	名	けが，負傷		**destroy**	動	壊す，打ち砕く
future	名	将来，未来		**tragic**	形	悲劇的な
no longer	熟	もはや～ない		**event**	名	出来事，事件
recovery	名	回復		thereby	副	それにより
along with ~	熟	~とともに，~と一緒に		**calling**	名	職業，天職
female	形	女性の		**not always**	熟	必ずしも～ない，いつも～す
vocalist	名	歌手				るわけではない
voice	名	声		**according to ~**		
trained	形	訓練された，熟練した			熟	~にしたがって，~のとおりに

example	名 例	**fulfilling**	形 充実した，やりがいのある
coincidental	形 偶然の	**unguessed**	形 予期できない，思いもよらない
circumstance	名 状況，出来事	**unsought**	形 望んでいない
lead *A* **to** *B*	熟 *A* を *B* に導く	**blessing**	名 (神の)恵み

第2段落　文の構造と語句のチェック

¹We make plans (expecting to be in control of what will happen).　²Perhaps
 S　V　　O

we fear natural happenings, things 〔 turning out contrary (to our wishes)〕.
 S　V　　　　O　　　└─同格─┘　　V′　　　　C′

³The course of life is challenging (if we are concerned (with trying to control
　　　　S　　　　　V　　C　　　従接 S　V　　　C

it)).　⁴We may act (with precision, and self-discipline), (expecting the world to
　　　　　S　　V　　　　　①　　等接　　②　　　　　　V′　　　O′

do the same and give us 〈 what we want 〉), but that is rarely the case.
C′　　　等接　　　　　関代　　　　　　　等接 S　V　　　　C

> **訳** ¹私たちは将来起こることをコントロールしようと期待して計画を立てる。²もしかする
> と私たちは自然の思いがけない出来事，つまり，結局自分の希望に反しているとわかるよ
> うな物事を恐れているのかもしれない。³人生の進路は，私たちが人生をコントロールしよ
> うとすることに関心があると，苦労を伴うものとなる。⁴私たちは正確さと自制心をもっ
> て，世間も(自分と)同じことをし，欲しいものを与えてくれると期待しながら行動するか
> もしれないが，そのようなことはめったにないのである。

Check! 第4文 We may act with precision, and self-discipline, expecting the
world to do the same and give us what we want, … の expecting は【付帯状況】
を表す分詞構文。「〜して，〜しながら」などと訳す。

語句

expect	動 期待する	**happening**	名 (思いがけない)出来事
▶ expect+O+to *do*		**turn out (to be)** 〜	
	熟 O が〜することを期待する		熟 結局〜になる，結局〜だとわかる
in control of 〜	熟 〜を支配〔管理，制御〕して	**contrary to** 〜	熟 〜と反対の，〜に反する
perhaps	副 ひょっとすると，もしかすると	**course**	名 進路，方向
		challenging	形 困難な，苦労を伴う

be concerned with ~		
	熟	~に関心を持っている
try to *do*	熟	~しようと試みる
act	動	行動する，ふるまう

precision	名	正確さ，精度
self-discipline	名	自己鍛錬，自制(心)
rarely	副	めったに~ない
be the case	熟	事実である，あてはまる

第3段落 文の構造と語句のチェック

¹Perfect discipline, or perfect control, is the most certain way [to miss out on
  S① 　　等接　　 S② 　　 V 　　　　 C

the joy of life]. ²The unexpectedness of life means ⟨ that we are free (not to
　　　　　　　　　 S 　　　　　　 V 　O 従接 S V 　C

plan perfectly)⟩. ³We can flow (into the natural chaos of life, so untidy, so
　　　　　　　　　 S 　V

unpredictable), or we can try to order life fully (by making careful plans).
　　　　　　 等接 S 　　 V 　　　　 O 　　　　　　　 V′ 　　　 O′

⁴But (as Rover Burns says), "The best-prepared schemes often go wrong and
等接 従接 　 S 　　 V 　　　　　　 S 　　　　　　　 V① C 　等接

leave us nothing but grief and pain [for promised joy]."
V② O₁ 　　　　　 O₂

> **訳** ¹完璧な統制，すなわち完璧なコントロールは，人生の喜びを逃してしまうもっとも確実な方法である。²人生の意外性とは，完全に計画を立てない自由があるということを意味する。³私たちは，非常に雑然として予測不可能な，人生の自然のままの混沌状態の中へ流れ込んでいくこともできるし，慎重な計画を立てることにより人生を完全に律しようとすることもできる。⁴しかし，ローバー・バーンズが述べているように，「もっとも用意周到な計画はしばしば失敗に終わり，私たちに残されるのは約束されていたはずの喜びに対する悲嘆と苦痛だけなのである」。

Check! 最終文 … and leave us nothing but grief and pain for promised joy の leave は第4文型の用法。〈leave＋O₁＋O₂〉で「O₁ に O₂ を残す」。ここでは us が O₁，nothing ～ joy が O₂ となる。

64

語句

discipline	名	規律，統制
certain	形	確実な
miss out on ～	熟	～（の機会）を逃す
unexpectedness	名	予想外であること
be free to *do*	熟	自由に～できる
flow into ～	熟	～に流れ込む
chaos	名	混沌，大混乱
untidy	形	乱れて，雑然として
unpredictable	形	予測不可能な

order	動	整える，整理する
fully	副	完全に，十分に
well-prepared	形	準備万端な，用意周到な
scheme	名	計画
go wrong	熟	うまくいかなくなる，失敗する
nothing but ～	熟	～だけ，～のみ
grief	名	悲しみ
pain	名	苦痛
promise	動	約束する
joy	名	喜び

第4段落　文の構造と語句のチェック

¹〈 Making plans 〉 is an adult occupation, a feature of a healthy ego. ²However,
　　S　　　　　　 V　　 C　　　　└─同格─┘

life often does not proceed （ according to our plans ）. ³This does not
S　　　　　 V

have to leave us disappointed. ⁴Perhaps we believe 〈 the universe has a plan
　　V　　　 O　 C　　　　　　　 S　 V　　　 S　　 V　 O
　　　　　　　　　　　　　　　　　　　　　┌─ 従接 that 省略

〔 that more accurately reflects our emerging destiny 〕〉.
関代　　　　　　　 V　　　 O

> **訳** ¹計画を立てることは大人の仕事であり，健全な自意識の特徴である。²しかし，人生は計画どおりに進まないことが多い。³そうだからといって私たちはがっかりする必要はない。⁴もしかすると私たちは，明らかになりつつある私たちの運命をより正確に反映する計画がこの世界にあるのだと，思い込んでいるのかもしれない。

Check! 第3文 This does not have to leave us disappointed. の leave は第5文型の用法。〈leave＋O＋C〉で「O を C の状態（のまま）にしておく」の意味。

語句

adult	形	大人の，大人びた
occupation	名	仕事
feature	名	特徴，特色
healthy	形	健全な，自然な
ego	名	自意識，自尊心
proceed	動	進む，進行する

disappointed	形	がっかりして，失望して
universe	名	宇宙，全世界
accurately	副	正確に
reflect	動	反映する
emerge	動	現れる，明らかになる
destiny	名	運命，宿命

文法事項の整理 ⑥　無生物主語

第1段落第2文の無生物主語についてみてみよう。

..., but **her injuries** made that future no longer possible.

主語が人間ではなく物事の場合，【無生物主語】という。そのような英文はいくらでもあるが，問題となるのは，直訳が不自然な場合である。例えば，次のような訳は，明らかに不自然である。

例　The heavy rain prevented us from going out.

（直訳）「大雨が私たちを外出することから妨げた」

そこで，「大雨のせいで私たちは外出できなかった」などと訳すことになる。

以上を整理すると，次のようになる。

無生物主語（＝S が物事）

直訳は不自然！　→　①英文の S を副詞的に訳す。

②可能な限り，人が主体となるように訳す。

ここで問題になるのが①であり，どのように「副詞的に」訳すのかを押さえておく必要がある。

■無生物主語の訳し方

	過去〜現在	現在〜未来
肯定文	（1）**because**	（3）**if**
否定文	（2）**though**	（4）**even if**

以下の例文で確認しよう（番号は表中のものと対応）。

（1）Hard work enabled him to succeed.

（直訳）「一生懸命働くことは，彼が成功することを可能にした」

▶ 過去形・肯定文なので **because** のイメージで訳す。

（意訳）「一生懸命働いたので，彼は成功できた」

(2) Hard work didn't enable him to succeed.

（直訳）「一生懸命働くことは，彼が成功することを可能にしなかった」

▶ 過去形・否定文なので though のイメージで訳す。

（意訳）「一生懸命働いたのだが，彼は成功できなかった」

(3) Hard work will enable him to succeed.

（直訳）「一生懸命働くことは，彼が成功することを可能にするであろう」

▶ 未来形・肯定文なので if のイメージで訳す。

（意訳）「もし一生懸命働けば，彼は成功できるだろう」

(4) Hard work won't enable him to succeed.

（直訳）「一生懸命働くことは，彼が成功することを可能にしないであろう」

▶ 未来形・否定文なので even if のイメージで訳す。

（意訳）「たとえ一生懸命働いても，彼は成功できないであろう」

（第 1 段落第 2 文）

..., but her injuries made that future no longer possible.

▶ 直訳すれば「彼女の負傷はそのような将来をもはや不可能にした」。左ページ表の(1)より，because のイメージで訳すと「彼女が負傷したため，そのような将来はもはや不可能となってしまった」となる。

（第 4 段落第 3 文）

This does not have to leave us disappointed.

▶ 直訳すれば「このことは私たちをがっかりさせておく必要はない」。表の(2)より，though のイメージで訳すと「そうであるが，私たちはがっかりする必要はない」となる。また，(4)より，even if のイメージで訳すと「たとえそうだとしても，私たちはがっかりする必要はない」となる（※時制が現在形の場合は，表の左右いずれの訳も可能。文脈に応じて適したほうを選ぶ）。

語句リストの復習

次の語句の意味を**ア~ト**からそれぞれ1つ選べ。

1	be involved in ~	11	fully
2	contrary to ~	12	scheme
3	injury	13	grief
4	tragic	14	destiny
5	recovery	15	circumstance
6	calling	16	original
7	hire	17	according to ~
8	feature	18	accurately
9	be concerned with ~	19	nothing but ~
10	discipline	20	graduation

ア	規律	サ	~に巻き込まれている
イ	卒業	シ	完全に
ウ	運命	ス	回復
エ	特徴	セ	正確に
オ	けが	ソ	最初の
カ	~だけ，~のみ	タ	天職
キ	~に関心を持っている	チ	計画
ク	雇う	ツ	悲劇的な
ケ	悲しみ	テ	~に従って
コ	~と反対の	ト	状況

答 1-サ 2-コ 3-オ 4-ツ 5-ス 6-タ 7-ク 8-エ 9-キ 10-ア
11-シ 12-チ 13-ケ 14-ウ 15-ト 16-ソ 17-テ 18-セ 19-カ 20-イ

ディクテーションしてみよう！ 🔊 27-30

今回学習した英文に出てきた単語を，音声を聞いて（　　　）に書き取ろう。

　　In the early 1940s, on the night of her graduation party, a high school girl named Doris Van Kappelhoff was ❶(i　　　　　) in a serious car accident. She had planned to go to Hollywood to become a dancer in films, but her injuries made that future no longer possible. During her long ❷(r　　　　　) at home, Doris began to sing along with the female vocalists on the radio. Her voice became so well trained that she was hired to sing in a band, and soon thereafter, she found parts in movies, changing her name to Doris

Day. Her original plans were destroyed by a ❸(t   ) event, but thereby she found her true calling. Things don't always go ❹(a   ) to our plans, but a change of plans may be an example of coincidental circumstances that lead us to a fulfilling life, unguessed and unsought — a blessing from God.

We make plans expecting to be in control of what will happen. Perhaps we fear natural happenings, things turning out ❺(c   ) to our wishes. The course of life is challenging if we are ❻(c   ) with trying to control it. We may act with precision, and self-discipline, expecting the world to do the same and give us what we want, but that is rarely the case.

Perfect discipline, or perfect control, is the most certain way to miss out on the joy of life. The unexpectedness of life means that we are free not to plan perfectly. We can flow into the natural chaos of life, so untidy, so unpredictable, or we can try to order life ❼(f   ) by making careful plans. But as Rover Burns says, "The best-prepared ❽(s   ) often go wrong and leave us nothing but ❾(g   ) and pain for promised joy."

Making plans is an adult occupation, a ❿(f   ) of a healthy ego. However, life often does not proceed according to our plans. This does not have to leave us disappointed. Perhaps we believe the universe has a plan that more accurately reflects our emerging ⓫(d   ).

答 ❶ involved   ❷ recovery   ❸ tragic   ❹ according   ❺ contrary   ❻ concerned
❼ fully   ❽ schemes   ❾ grief   ❿ feature   ⓫ destiny

解答

問1 （ア）	①	（イ）	③	（ウ）	②
問2 （エ）	④	（オ）	②	（カ）	①

解説

問1

（ア） **in order to** *do* で「**～するために**」の意味。【**目的**】を表す。なお，②の with regard to ～ や④の with reference to ～ は「～に関して」の意味だが，「～」の部分は名詞なので，ここでは文法的にも不可。

（イ） **on the contrary** は「**それどころか**」の意味で，前の内容を修正して言い直す時に使う。

> 例　The results were not bad; <u>on the contrary</u>, they showed great improvement.
> 「結果は悪くなかった。それどころか，大幅に改善が見られた」

ここでは，「問題はない→それどころか→好印象で有利になる」という流れ。他の選択肢の意味は，①「しかし」，②「さらに，その上」，④「その結果」。

（ウ） 好印象を与えるための条件を列挙している文脈。直後の文に It is also very important … とあるので，**（ウ）**を含む文はこれと類似した内容になるはず。② essential は「非常に重要な，必要不可欠な」（≒very important）という意味で，これが正解。他の選択肢の意味は，①「正式な」，③「純粋な，本物の」，④「正当な，有効な」。

問2

（エ） 「就職活動に関する本は＿＿＿＿＿」
① 「読むのがつらい」
② 「雇用者になりそうな人を列挙している」
③ 「人々を緊張させる」
④ **「役に立つ手引きを与えてくれる」**
▶ ④が第1段落第2，3文と一致。

（オ）「求職者は＿＿＿＿＿＿＿すべきだ」

① 「事前に到着した場合，何者か知られるのは避ける」

② **「道に迷うのを避けるため１日早くオフィスを訪れる」**

③ 「頭が良いと思われるために，約束の時間を過ぎてから到着する」

④ 「従業員の衣服や行動について自分の考えを述べる」

▶ ②が第２段落第３文と一致。

（カ）「良い第一印象を与えることは重要である。なぜなら＿＿＿＿＿＿＿」

① **「管理職の人は採用の決断を非常に素早く行うから」**

② 「志願者はちゃんとした服装をし，興味を持っているから」

③ 「面接官は誠実な『アイコンタクト』に感銘を受けるから」

④ 「志願者はその他の点では良くない反応をするから」

▶ ①が第３段落第１文と一致。③については第３段落最終文に「目を見ること」が重要である理由として挙げられている。

それでは次に，段落ごとに詳しくみていこう。　🔊 31

第１段落　文の構造と語句のチェック

1〈 Hunting for a job 〉 is a painful experience, but one 〔 that nearly everyone must endure (at least once) (in a lifetime)〕. 2Books are published and magazine articles are written (on the subject), (all trying to tell job-seekers 〈 what they should do or avoid doing (in order to survive and to win the game)〉).
— should 省略

3They can't calm the nervous applicant (and what applicant is not nervous?), but they do offer some advice 〔 that deserves consideration 〕.

訳 ¹就職活動は苦痛な経験であるが，ほぼすべての人が一生に少なくとも一度は耐えなくてはならない経験である。²そのテーマに関して様々な本が出版され，雑誌の記事が書かれており，いずれも求職者に対し，生き残ってゲームに勝つためにすべきこと，あるいはするのを避けるべきことを伝えようとしている。³それらは緊張している求職者を落ち着かせることはできない（そして，どんな応募者が緊張していないというのだろうか）が，考慮に値する助言を実際に提供してくれているのだ。

Check! 第1文 Hunting for a job is a painful experience, but one that nearly everyone must endure at least once in a lifetime. の one は an experience の代用となる代名詞。that は目的格の関係代名詞で，endure の後に O が欠けている。

語句

hunt for ~	熟	~を探し求める
painful	形	つらい，苦痛な
experience	名	経験
nearly	副	ほとんど，ほぼ
endure	動	耐える，我慢する
at least	熟	少なくとも
lifetime	名	一生，生涯
publish	動	出版する
article	名	記事
subject	名	主題，テーマ
job-seeker	名	求職者，就職希望者
avoid	動	避ける
in order to *do*	熟	~するために
survive	動	生き残る
calm	動	落ち着かせる，なだめる
nervous	形	緊張して
applicant	名	応募者，志願者
offer	動	提供する
deserve	動	値する
consideration	名	考慮

第2段落　文の構造と語句のチェック

¹(To begin with), it is not a good idea 〈 to be late 〉. ²Job interviewers
　　　　　　　　　　　仮S V　　C　　　　真S

don't think very highly of the candidate 〔 who arrives (twenty minutes after the
　　　　V　　　　　　　　　　　O　　　　　関代　V

appointed time), (offering no apology) or (explaining 〈 that he couldn't find
　　　　　　　　　　①V'　　O'　　　等接　②V'　　従接 O'① S　V

the street 〉, and 〈 that his watch is slow 〉)〕. ³The wise job-seeker explores
　　O　　等接　　従接 O'② S　V C　　　　　　S　　　　V

72

the place (the day before) (to make sure ⟨ that he can locate the building,
　　O　　　　　　　　　　　　　　　　V′　　　　O′従接　S　　V　　　　O①

the right floor, and the office 〔 in which the interview is to take place 〕⟩); (at
　O②　　　　等接　　O③　　　関代　　　　S　　　　　V

the same time) he looks around (to see ⟨ what the employees are wearing ⟩ and
　　　　　　　　　S　　V　　　　　　　V′　　疑　O′①　　S　　　　V　　　等接

⟨ how they seem to behave (at work)⟩). ⁴(Next day) he arrives (early for the
　疑　S　　V　　　　　　　　　　　　　　　　　　　　　　　　S　　V

appointment). ⁵It does not matter (if the employer's secretary recognizes him
　　　　　　　　　S　　V　　　　従接　　　　S　　　　　　V①　　　O

and mentions his first visit (to her boss)). ⁶(On the contrary), the eager
等接　V②　　　O　　　　　　　　　　　　　　　　　　　　　　　　　S

candidate can only be regarded (as smart, thoughtful, and well-organized) —
　S　　　　　V　　　　　　　①　　　②　　　等接　　③

three points in his favor (before he has said a word).
　　　　　　　　　　　　従接　S　　V　　　O

訳 ¹まず第一に，遅刻をするのは良い考えではない。²就職の面接官は，約束の時間の20分後に到着し，謝罪もせず，あるいは道がわからなかったとか時計が遅れていたなどと釈明をするような志願者のことは，あまり高く評価しない。³賢明な求職者は前日に，面接が行われる予定の建物，正しい階，オフィスを確実に見つけられるよう，場所を調査する。同時に，従業員が何を着ているか，そして彼らが仕事中にどのような行動をしているように思われるかを確かめるために，見て回る。⁴翌日は約束のために早めに到着する。⁵雇用者の秘書がその人に見覚えがあって，最初の訪問について上司に言ったとしても問題ない。⁶それどころか，その熱意ある志願者は，頭が良く，思慮深く，几帳面であると見てもらえるだけである。つまり，一言も発しないうちに３つの点が有利に働くのだ。

Check! 第3文 … and the office in which the interview is to take place の is to は「〜する予定である」の意味。be to do は【義務】【予定】【運命】【可能】【意図】などの意味を持つ。

Check! 第 5 文 It does not matter if the employer's secretary recognizes him … の if は副詞節を導き，「たとえ…しても」（≒even if）の意味。It は形式主語（仮主語）ではなく，後続の if 節の内容を指す。

例 I'd appreciate it if you would help me.
「手伝っていただけるならありがたいのですが」

語句

to begin with	熟 最初に，まず第一に	seem to *do*	熟 ～するように思われる
interviewer	名 面接官，面接担当者	behave	動 ふるまう，行動する
think highly of ~		at work	熟 仕事中に，職場で
	熟 ～を高く評価する，～を重視する	appointment	名 （面会の）約束，予約
candidate	名 志願者，志望者	matter	動 重要である，問題となる
appointed	形 指定された，約束の	employer	名 雇い主，雇用者
apology	名 謝罪	secretary	名 秘書
explain	動 説明する	recognize	動 （人の）顔を覚えている，見覚えがある
explore	動 調査する		
the day before	副 前日（に）	mention	動 言及する，述べる
make sure that ...		boss	名 上司
	熟 …ということを確認する，確実にする	on the contrary	熟 それどころか，反対に
locate	動 （場所を）見つける	eager	形 熱心な，熱意のある
interview	名 面接	regard *A* as *B*	熟 A を B とみなす
take place	熟 行われる，起こる	smart	形 賢明な，頭の良い
at the same time	熟 同時に	thoughtful	形 思慮深い
look around	熟 周囲を見回す，見て回る	well-organized	
employee	名 従業員		形 （人が）きちんとした，几帳面な
		in *one*'s favor	熟 ～に有利で

第 3 段落　文の構造と語句のチェック

[1]Most personnel managers admit ⟨ that they know (within the first few

minutes of the meeting) ⟨ whether or not they want to hire the person [to

whom they are talking]⟩⟩. [2]This is particularly true (when their first reaction

〔 to the applicant 〕 is negative), (when the man or woman has made a

disastrous first impression). ³But what makes a *good* impression? ⁴What

counts? ⁵〈 Being on time 〉 does, (as we have seen); then, appearance. ⁶It is

essential 〈 for the candidate to be dressed properly, and to look alert,

pleasant, and interested 〉. ⁷It is also very important 〈 to look the interviewer

(in the eyes)〉(because this "eye contact" gives a strong impression 〔 of

sincerity and openness 〕).

訳 ¹ほとんどの人事部長は，会ってから最初の数分以内に，自分が話している人物を採用したいかどうかわかると認める。²これは，応募者に対する最初の反応が良くなかったり，その男性または女性がひどい第一印象を与えてしまった場合には，特にそうである。³しかし，何が「良い」印象を作り出すのだろうか。⁴何が重要なのだろうか。⁵ここまでに見てきたように，時間に正確であるということは，確かにあてはまる。次に，外見である。⁶志願者は適切な服装をし，機敏で愛想が良く興味を持っているように見えることが不可欠である。⁷また，面接官の目をしっかり見ることも非常に重要である。なぜなら，こういう「アイコンタクト」は誠実で心が広いという強い印象を与えるからだ。

Check! 第1文 … they know within the first few minutes of the meeting whether or not they want to hire the person to whom they are talking. の V が know，O は whether 以下。この場合の whether は名詞節の用法で「…かどうか」の意味。V と O の間に前置詞句(within the first few minutes of the meeting)が挟まっている。なお，whether の後の or not は節の最後に置くこともあり，省略可能で，なくても意味は変わらない。

Check! 第5文の does は代動詞で，第4文の counts の代用。appearance の後にも同様の does が省略されていると考えてよい。

personnel	名	人事（部）		**count**	動	重要である
manager	名	部長，主任		**appearance**	名	外見
admit	動	認める		**essential**	形	必要不可欠の，重要な
within	前	～のうちに，範囲内で		**dress**	動	衣服を身につける
hire	動	雇う		**properly**	副	適切に
particularly	副	特に		**alert**	形	油断のない，機敏な
reaction	名	反応		**pleasant**	形	愛想の良い，好感の持てる
negative	形	否定的な，マイナスの		**look ~ in the eye(s)**		
disastrous	形	ひどい，悲惨な			熟	～（人）の目をじっと見る
impression	名	印象		**sincerity**	名	誠実さ，誠意
				openness	名	心の広さ，開放性

文法事項の整理 ⑦　強調の do

第 1 段落最終文の do についてみてみよう。

..., but they **do** offer some advice that deserves consideration

〈do [does / did]＋原形〉は動詞の【強調】を表す。「確かに，実際，本当に（～する）」などと訳す。また，命令文の場合は「ぜひ～しなさい」と訳す。

例　He *does* understand what you said.
「彼はあなたが言ったことをちゃんと理解していますよ」

例　"You didn't say that." "I *did* say that!"
「君はそんなことは言わなかったよ」「いや，確かに言った！」

例　*Do* come to see us.
「ぜひ会いにいらっしゃい」

（第 1 段落最終文）

..., but they do offer some advice that deserves consideration
▶ do が offer を強調している。

語句リストの復習

次の語句の意味を**ア**〜**ト**からそれぞれ１つ選べ。

/20点

1	experience	11	mention
2	interview	12	smart
3	endure	13	reaction
4	applicant	14	sincerity
5	publish	15	explore
6	consideration	16	subject
7	article	17	apology
8	appearance	18	essential
9	appointment	19	admit
10	secretary	20	painful

ア	必要不可欠の	サ	主題
イ	耐える	シ	経験
ウ	秘書	ス	言及する
エ	賢明な	セ	出版する
オ	誠実さ	ソ	外見
カ	反応	タ	認める
キ	調査する	チ	応募者
ク	（面会の）約束	ツ	つらい
ケ	面接	テ	記事
コ	謝罪	ト	考慮

答 1―シ 2―ケ 3―イ 4―チ 5―セ 6―ト 7―テ 8―ソ 9―ク 10―ウ
11―ス 12―エ 13―カ 14―オ 15―キ 16―サ 17―コ 18―ア 19―タ 20―ツ

ディクテーションしてみよう！ 32-34

今回学習した英文に出てきた単語を，音声を聞いて（　　）に書き取ろう。

Hunting for a job is a painful **❶**(e   ), but one
that nearly everyone must endure at least once in a lifetime. Books
are **❷**(p   ) and magazine articles are written on the
subject, all trying to tell job-seekers what they should do or avoid
doing in order to survive and to win the game. They can't calm the
nervous applicant (and what applicant is not nervous?), but they do
offer some advice that deserves consideration.

　　To begin with, it is not a good idea to be late. Job interviewers
don't think very highly of the candidate who arrives twenty minutes

after the appointed time, offering no ❸(a   ) or explaining that he couldn't find the street, and that his watch is slow. The wise job-seeker explores the place the day before to make sure that he can locate the building, the right floor, and the office in which the interview is to take place; at the same time he looks around to see what the employees are wearing and how they seem to behave at work. Next day he arrives early for the ❹(a   ). It does not matter if the employer's ❺(s   ) recognizes him and mentions his first visit to her boss. On the contrary, the eager candidate can only be regarded as smart, thoughtful, and well-organized — three points in his favor before he has said a word.

Most personnel managers ❻(a   ) that they know within the first few minutes of the meeting whether or not they want to hire the person to whom they are talking. This is particularly true when their first ❼(r   ) to the applicant is negative, when the man or woman has made a disastrous first impression. But what makes a *good* impression? What counts? Being on time does, as we have seen; then, ❽(a   ). It is ❾(e   ) for the candidate to be dressed properly, and to look alert, pleasant, and interested. It is also very important to look the interviewer in the eyes because this "eye contact" gives a strong impression of sincerity and openness.

答 ❶ experience ❷ published ❸ apology ❹ appointment ❺ secretary ❻ admit
❼ reaction ❽ appearance ❾ essential

解答

問1	1年半もたたないうちに，フィリスは英語が流ちょうになっており，（それ以前から）ラテン語も学び始めていた。

問2	Phillis Wheatley

問3	（ア）born	（ウ）taught	（オ）assigned	（カ）Treated

問4	（イ）②	（ク）①	（ケ）①	（コ）②	（サ）②

問5	① ×	② ×	③ ○	④ ×	⑤ ×	⑥ ×	⑦ ○

解説

問1 以下のポイントをおさえよう！

☑ **within** は前置詞で「**～以内に，～もたたないうちに**」の意味。

☑ a year and a half は「1年半」。

☑ had also begun は過去完了形なので，1年半が経過するまでに，すでにラテン語を学び始めていたことになる。

問2

下線部の意味は「非常に並外れた女性の奴隷」。extraordinary は「並外れた，ずば抜けた」の意味。第1段落第1，2文から，フィリス・ウィートリーが女性の奴隷であったことがわかる。また，第1段落後半と第2段落前半から，フィリス・ウィートリーが詩を作ることで有名になったこともわかる。

問3

（ア） bear「生む」の活用は **bear-bore-born [borne]**。【受動】を表す過去分詞の borne は，直後に by ～（生んだ人）が続く場合のみ用いる。

> 例　He is the only child **borne** by the lady.
> 「彼はその女性が生んだ唯一の子だ」

それ以外の場合は **be born** で「生まれる」の意味。

（ウ） When から始まる副詞節が終わった後なので，**（ウ）** を含む文は主節である。時制は過去形が適切。teach の活用は **teach-taught-taught**。

(オ) assign は「割り当てる，課す」の意味。ここでは role「役割」を修飾するので，「課された役割」と考えて，**【受動】**を表す過去分詞にする。

(カ) **treat A as B** で**「A を B として扱う」**。A にあたる目的語がないこと，また後ろに by があることに注目し，受動態を表す過去分詞にする。ここでは直前に Being が省略された分詞構文（**【付帯状況】**を表すと考えてよい）となっている。

問4

(イ) 直前に，奴隷船でアメリカに来てボストンで買われたとの内容があるので，servant「召使い」が適切。

(ク) 空所の前に returned to「～へ戻ってきた」とあるので，イギリスに旅行する前にどこにいたのかを考える。第1段落第2文参照。

(ケ) 第2段落後半にはイギリスの王室に招かれたこと，第3段落にはベンジャミン・フランクリンやジョージ・ワシントンの目にとまったことが書かれているので，国際的な「名声」を得たと考える。選択肢の意味は，①「名声」，②「自由」，③「旅行」。achieve fame で「名声を得る」。

(コ) 奴隷であったフィリスが解放されたとの記述が第2段落最終文にあるが，最終段落第2文には解放後も主人のもとで暮らしたとあるので，解放されたことを特に喜んでいないとするのが文脈に合う。選択肢の意味は，①「活動」，②「解放」，③「奴隷制」。

(サ) the beloved（　　）となっているので，空所には名詞が入る。よって，①は不可（liberate は「～を解放する」の意味の動詞）。また，than の前の as a free black woman との対比を考えると，③も不自然。

問5

① 「フィリスは 17 世紀なかばにアメリカに来た」
▶ 第1段落第2文と不一致。1761 年は 18 世紀。

② 「ウィートリー夫妻には子供がおらず，フィリスを我が子と思っていた」
▶ 第1段落第3文と不一致。ウィートリー夫妻には娘がいたことがわかる。

③ 「フィリスはアメリカに来た時，英語が得意ではなかった」
▶ 第1段落第3文に，ウィートリー夫妻の娘が（英語の）読み方を教えたとの記述があるので，当初は英語が不得手であったと判断できる。

④「フィリスはニューイングランドの新聞社で働いた」

▶ 第1段落第6文と不一致。作品が新聞に掲載されたのであって，新聞社に勤務したわけではない。本文の work は「著作，作品」の意味。

⑤「フィリスはいい召使いだったのだが，ウィートリー一家は彼女をあまり気に入っていなかった」

▶ 第2段落第1文に娘のように扱われたこと，第4段落第2文に beloved「愛された」とあることと矛盾する。

⑥「ウィートリー夫人はフィリスを死の間際に解放した」

▶ 第2段落最終文によれば，フィリスを解放したのは夫のジョン・ウィートリーである。

⑦ **「アメリカでは独立を求めて戦った黒人もいた」**

▶ 第3段落最後の2文と一致。

それでは次に，段落ごとに詳しくみていこう。　🔊 35

第1段落　文の構造と語句のチェック

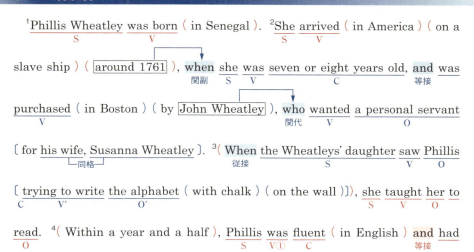

also begun to study Latin. ⁵(By the time she was thirteen) she was writing
　　　　　　V②　　　 O　　　　　　従接　　　S　V　C　　　S　　V

poetry. ⁶Her work began to appear (in New England newspapers), and she
 O　　　　　 S　　　 V　　　　　　　　　　　　　　　　　　 等接　S

became a regional celebrity. ⁷She had found a way 〔 out of the normal
 V　　　 C　　　　　　　　　　　 S　　 V　　 O

restrictions 〔 of her assigned role 〔 in life 〕〕〕(through poetry).

訳 ¹フィリス・ウィートリーはセネガルで生まれた。²彼女は7歳か8歳で1761年頃に奴隷船でアメリカに到着し，ボストンでジョン・ウィートリーに買われた。彼は妻のスザンナ・ウィートリーのための個人的な召使いを求めていたのだった。³ウィートリー夫妻の娘が，フィリスが壁にチョークでアルファベットを書こうとしているのを見かけたとき，フィリスに読み方を教えてあげた。⁴1年半もたたないうちに，フィリスは英語が流ちょうになっており，（それ以前から）ラテン語も学び始めていた。⁵13歳になるまでには詩を書いていた。⁶彼女の作品はニューイングランドの新聞に掲載されるようになり，彼女は地域の有名人になった。⁷彼女は詩を通じて，人生において課された役割の通常の制約から脱する道を見つけたのだ。

語 句

bear	動	生む

▶活用：bear-bore-born [borne]

slave	名	奴隷
purchase	動	買う，購入する
personal	形	個人の，私的な
servant	名	使用人，召使い
daughter	名	娘
try to *do*	熟	～しようとする
alphabet	名	アルファベット
chalk	名	チョーク
within	前	～以内に，～もたたないうちに
fluent	形	流ちょうな
Latin	名	ラテン語
by the time ...	熟	…する時までに
poetry	名	詩，詩歌
work	名	著作，作品
appear	動	載る，掲載される
regional	形	地域の，地方の
celebrity	名	有名人
normal	形	普通の
restriction	名	制限，制約
assign	動	割り当てる，課す
role	名	役割

第2段落　文の構造と語句のチェック

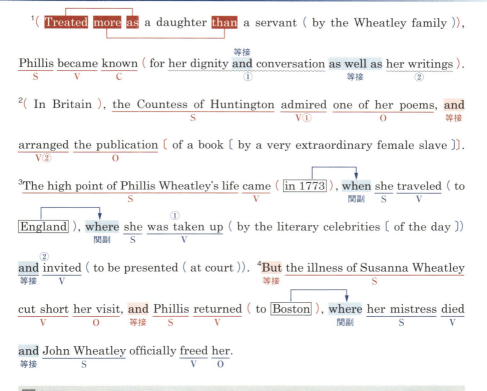

> 訳 ¹ウィートリー家からは召使いというよりむしろ娘として扱われ，フィリスは著作物だけでなく気品の高さや交友でも知られるようになった。²イギリスではハンティントン伯爵夫人が彼女の詩の1つを賞賛し，非常に並外れた女性の奴隷による本の出版を手配した。³フィリス・ウィートリーの人生の頂点は1773年にめぐってきた。その年，彼女はイングランドへと旅行し，そこで当時の文学界の著名人達に支援され，宮廷で正式に紹介を受けるよう招かれた。⁴しかし，スザンナ・ウィートリーが病気になったため，彼女のイングランド訪問は早めに切り上げられ，フィリスはボストンに戻った。ボストンでは彼女の女主人が亡くなり，ジョン・ウィートリーは正式に彼女を自由の身にしてやった。

語句		
treat *A* **as** *B*	熟	AをBとして扱う
more *A* **than** *B*	熟	BというよりむしろA
dignity	名	品位，気品
conversation	名	交際，社交
A **as well as** *B*	熟	BだけでなくAも
writing	名	著作，（書いた）作品
countess	名	伯爵夫人

admire	動	賞賛する	invite	動	招待する，招く
poem	名	詩	present	動	(正式に)紹介する，引き合わ
arrange	動	手配する，準備する			せる
publication	名	出版	court	名	宮廷，王宮
extraordinary	形	並外れた，ずば抜けた	cut short ~	熟	~を切り上げる，早めに終える
female	形	女性の	mistress	名	(女性の)主人，所有者
take up ~	熟	~を支援する，援助する	officially	副	正式に，公式に
literary	形	文学の	free	動	解放する，自由にする
of the day	熟	当時の，その時代の			

第3段落　文の構造と語句のチェック

¹She was the first American writer 〔 to achieve international fame 〕.
S　V　　　　　　C

²Benjamin Franklin read her work, which sometimes compared the experience of
S　　　　　　V　　O　　関代　　　　　V　　　　　O

a slave (to that 〔 of American colonists 〔 under British tyranny 〕)). ³George
‖
the experience

Washington invited her (to visit him (at his camp) (during the War of
S　　　　V　　O

Independence)). ⁴Some historians credit her (with Washington's decision 〔 to
S　　　　　V　　O

allow black men to serve in his army 〕).
V′　　O′　　　　C′

> 訳 ¹彼女は国際的な名声を獲得した最初のアメリカ人作家であった。²ベンジャミン・フランクリンは彼女の作品を読んだが，その作品は時に奴隷の経験をイギリスの圧政下におけるアメリカ人開拓者の経験にたとえるものであった。³ジョージ・ワシントンは独立戦争中，彼女を野営地の彼のもとに来るよう招いた。⁴歴史家の中には，ワシントンが黒人の従軍を許可する決断をしたのは彼女の功績であると考える者もいる。

語句

achieve	動	獲得する，得る	compare A to B	熟	A を B にたとえる
international	形	国際的な	experience	名	経験
fame	名	名声	colonist	名	(植民地)開拓者，入植者
			tyranny	名	暴政，圧政

84

camp	名 野営地	decision	名 決意, 決断
the War of Independence		allow	動 許可する
	名 (アメリカ)独立戦争	serve	動 仕える, 奉仕する
historian	名 歴史家	army	名 軍隊
credit *A* with *B*	熟 A(人)にBの功績があると考える		

第4段落　文の構造と語句のチェック

¹Phillis Wheatley found no happiness (in her own liberty). ²She continued to
　S　　　　　　V　　　O　　　　　　　　　　　　　　　　S　　　　V

live (with her old master) (until his death), but the people of Boston had
V　　　　　　　　　　　　　　　　　　　　　　　　　等接　　　S　　　　　V

much less interest (in her) (as a free black woman) than they did (when she
　　　　　O　　　　　　　　　　　　　　　　　　　　　　　　　　S　V　従接　S

was the beloved slave 〔 of a prominent white family 〕).
V　　　　　C

> **訳** ¹フィリス・ウィートリーは自らの解放をうれしく思うことはなかった。²彼女は元の主人が死ぬまで彼とともに暮らし続けた。しかし，ボストンの人々は解放された黒人女性としてよりむしろ，有名な白人家庭の愛される奴隷であった時に，はるかに高い関心を彼女に対して示した。

語句

happiness	名 幸福, 喜び	death	名 死
liberty	名 自由, 解放	less *A* than *B*	熟 AよりむしろB
continue to *do*	熟 ～し続ける	beloved	形 愛される
master	名 (男性の)主人	prominent	形 有名な

85

文法事項の整理 ⑧　関係詞の非制限用法

第1段落第2文の when についてみてみよう。

She arrived in America on a slave ship around 1761, **when** she was seven or eight years old, ...

　　これは前の名詞（先行詞）を補足説明する関係詞の【非制限用法】と呼ばれるものである。関係代名詞，関係副詞それぞれに非制限用法がある。

■関係代名詞の非制限用法
　　「制限用法」の関係代名詞は普通，前の名詞（先行詞）を修飾するので，和訳するときも後ろから訳す。

　　例　He has two brothers who work in this office.
　　　　「彼にはこの会社で働いている2人の兄弟がいる」

　　これに対し，「非制限用法」の関係代名詞は，＜, (コンマ)＋関係代名詞＞の形で，先行詞について補足説明をする。和訳するときは，前から訳す。

　　例　He has two brothers, who work in this office.
　　　　「彼には2人の兄弟がいて，その2人はこの会社で働いている」

＊訳し方は，文脈に応じ，「〜, そして…」「〜, しかし…」「〜, だから…」「〜, なぜなら…」などとする。

　　＜, (コンマ)＋which＞は前の名詞だけでなく，主節（の一部）を指すことができる。

　　例　I tried to read the book, which was written in easy English.
　　　　「私はその本を読もうとした。それは易しい英語で書かれていたからだ」
　　　▶ which は the book を指す。

　　例　I tried to read the book, which I found impossible.
　　　　「私はその本を読もうとしたが，それが無理だとわかった」
　　　▶ which は to read the book を指す。

例 I tried to read the book, which surprised our teacher.
「私はその本を読もうとしたが，そのことで先生はびっくりした」
▶ which は I tried to read the book という主節全体を指す。

■関係副詞の非制限用法

「制限用法」の関係副詞も，普通は前の名詞（先行詞）を修飾するので，和訳するときも後ろから訳す。

例 Tokyo is one of the cities where I want to live some day.
「東京はいつか住んでみたい都市の1つだ」

これに対し，**「非制限用法」**の関係副詞は＜，（コンマ）＋関係副詞＞の形で，先行詞について補足説明をすることができる。和訳するときは，前から訳す。なお，この用法を持つ関係副詞は **when** と **where のみ**である。

例 I want to visit Kyoto, where there are many old temples and shrines.
「私は京都に行ってみたい。そこには多くの古い寺や神社があるからだ」

（第1段落第2文）
She arrived in America on a slave ship around 1761, when she was seven or eight years old, and was purchased in Boston by John Wheatley, who wanted a personal servant for his wife, Susanna Wheatley.
▶ when は関係副詞の非制限用法で around 1761 についての補足説明。who は関係代名詞の非制限用法で，John Wheatley についての補足説明。なお，先行詞が固有名詞の場合，制限用法は不可で，必ず非制限用法になる。

（第2段落第3文）
The high point of Phillis Wheatley's life came in 1773, when she traveled to England, where she was taken up by the literary celebrities of the day and invited to be presented at court.
▶ when は関係副詞の非制限用法で in 1773 についての補足説明。where も関係副詞の非制限用法で，England についての補足説明。

（第2段落第4文）

But the illness of Susanna Wheatley cut short her visit, and Phillis returned to Boston, where her mistress died and John Wheatley officially freed her.

▶ where は関係副詞の非制限用法で Boston についての補足説明。

（第3段落第2文）

Benjamin Franklin read her work, which sometimes compared the experience of a slave to that of American colonists under British tyranny.

▶ which は関係代名詞の非制限用法で，her work についての補足説明。

語句リストの復習

次の語句の意味をア～トからそれぞれ1つ選べ。

/20点

1	purchase	11	fame
2	literary	12	compare A to B
3	fluent	13	serve
4	dignity	14	prominent
5	regional	15	extraordinary
6	admire	16	treat A as B
7	restriction	17	publication
8	army	18	liberty
9	officially	19	tyranny
10	achieve	20	slave

ア	品位	シ	有名な
イ	自由	ス	仕える
ウ	獲得する	セ	正式に
エ	並外れた	ソ	軍隊
オ	制限	タ	A を B として扱う
カ	暴政		
キ	賞賛する	チ	地域の
ク	奴隷	ツ	流ちょうな
ケ	文学の	テ	A を B にたとえる
コ	出版		
サ	買う	ト	名声

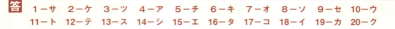

答 1—サ 2—ケ 3—ツ 4—ア 5—チ 6—キ 7—オ 8—ソ 9—セ 10—ウ
11—ト 12—テ 13—ス 14—シ 15—エ 16—タ 17—コ 18—イ 19—カ 20—ク

ディクテーションしてみよう！ 🔊 36-39

今回学習した英文に出てきた単語を，音声を聞いて（　　　）に書き取ろう。

Phillis Wheatley was born in Senegal. She arrived in America on a slave ship around 1761, when she was seven or eight years old, and was **❶**(p　　　　　　) in Boston by John Wheatley, who wanted a personal servant for his wife, Susanna Wheatley. When the Wheatleys' daughter saw Phillis trying to write the alphabet with chalk on the wall, she taught her to read. Within a year and a half, Phillis was **❷**(f　　　　) in English and had also begun to study Latin. By the time she was thirteen she was writing poetry. Her work began to appear in New England newspapers, and she became a **❸**(r　　　　　) celebrity. She had found a way out of the normal **❹**(r　　　　　) of her assigned role in life through poetry.

Treated more as a daughter than a servant by the Wheatley family, Phillis became known for her **❺**(d　　　　) and conversation as well as her writings. In Britain, the Countess of Huntington **❻**(a　　　　) one of her poems, and arranged the publication of a book by a very extraordinary female slave. The high point of Phillis Wheatley's life came in 1773, when she traveled to England, where she was taken up by the **❼**(l　　　　　) celebrities of the day and invited to be presented at court. But the illness of Susanna Wheatley cut short her visit, and Phillis returned to Boston, where her mistress died and John Wheatley officially freed her.

She was the first American writer to **❽**(a　　　　　) international **❾**(f　　) . Benjamin Franklin read her work, which sometimes compared the experience of a slave to that of American colonists under British tyranny. George Washington invited her to visit him at his camp during the War of Independence. Some historians credit her with Washington's decision to allow black men to **⑩**(s   ) in his army.

Phillis Wheatley found no happiness in her own **⑪** (l   ). She continued to live with her old master until his death, but the people of Boston had much less interest in her as a free black woman than they did when she was the beloved slave of a prominent white family.

解 答

問1	（ア）	②	（イ）	②	（ウ）	①	（エ）	①	（オ）	③
問2	①	×	②	○	③	○	④	×	⑤	×

解 説

問1

（ア） 選択肢は，① steam「蒸す，ふかす」，② grind「挽いて粉にする」，③ peel「（皮を）むく」。目的語が corn（小麦などの穀物）であり，風力を使うということから判断する。また，直後の部分で windmill「風車」という語の語源になっているとの記述があり，mill は「製粉所」の意味なので，これもヒントになる。

（イ）「上部にプロペラが付いている塔」という意味にするのが自然。with は「〜のある，〜が付いている」という【付属・存在】の意味をもつ。

（ウ） 目的語が many of these towers である点，副詞の together「（同じ場所に）一緒に」があることから考える。

（エ） at the top of 〜 で「〜のてっぺん［頂上］に」の意味。at は【点・地点】を表す前置詞。

（オ） farms「農場」は Isolated places「孤立した場所」の具体例。***A such as B [such A as B]*「B のような A」**において，B は A の具体例となる。

問2

① 「ヨーロッパ人が初めて農業において風力を利用した」

▶ 第1段落第2，3文と不一致。the Middle Ages「中世」よりも 4,000 年前の方が古い。

② **「風が起こる原因は空気中の場所によって気温が異なることにある」**

▶ 第2段落第1，2文と一致。

③ **「風力発電地帯は，風がより強い場所に建設される」**

▶ 第2段落最終文と一致。

④ 「ほとんどの風力発電地帯は沖合にある」

▶ 第3段落第2文と不一致。「ほとんど」とは書かれていない。

⑤ 「垂直のタービンは風の方を向くように発電機とプロペラを回転させる」

▶ 第4段落第3文と不一致。

それでは次に，段落ごとに詳しくみていこう。 🔊 40

第1段落　文の構造と語句のチェック

¹We've used the wind (as an energy source) (for a long time). ²The
　S　　　V　　　O

Babylonians and Chinese were using wind power (to pump water 〔 for
　①　等接　②　S　　　　　V　　　　O

irrigating crops 〕) (4,000 years ago), and sailing boats were around (long
　　　　　　　　　　　　　　　等接　　S　　　V　　　C

before that). ³Wind power was used (in the Middle Ages), (in Europe), (to
　　　　　　　　S　　　　V

grind corn), which is 〈 where the term "windmill" comes from 〉.
　　　　　関代 V C 関副　　　S　　　　　　　　V

> 訳 ¹私たちは長い間，風をエネルギー源として使ってきた。²バビロニア人や中国人は4,000年前に農作物に水を引くための水をくみ上げるのに風力を使っていたし，帆船はそのずっと前にあった。³中世のヨーロッパでも風力は穀物を粉にするために使われており，それがwindmill（風車）という語の由来である。

Check! 第3文 Wind power was used in the Middle Ages, in Europe, to grind corn, which is where the term "windmill" comes from. のwhichは**【非制限用法】**の関係代名詞。主節全体の内容を受ける用法（→ p.86 参照）。またwhereは関係副詞で，先行詞が省略されている。

語句

source	名	源，供給源
▶ energy source	名	エネルギー源
for a long time	熟	長い間
pump	動	（ポンプで）くみ上げる，注入する
irrigate	動	水を引く
crop	名	農作物

sailing boat	名	帆船，ヨット
around	副	存在して，出回って
grind	動	すりつぶす，粉にする
corn	名	穀物(小麦，トウモロコシなど)
term	名	言葉，用語
windmill	名	風車
come from ～	熟	～に由来する

第2段落 文の構造と語句のチェック

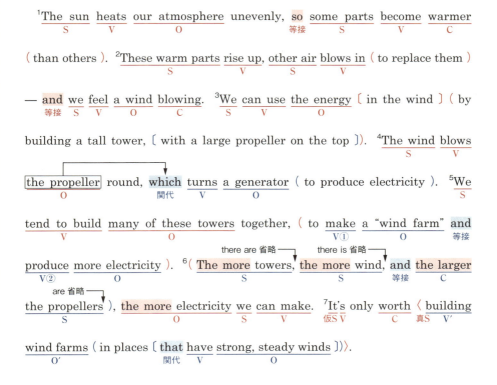

訳 ¹太陽は私たちの大気を不均等に温めるので，ある部分が別の部分より温かくなる。²この温かい部分が上昇し，他の空気がそれに取って代わろうと吹き込んでくる。そしてそのことで私たちは風が吹いていると感じるのだ。³私たちは風のエネルギーを，てっぺんに大きなプロペラのついた高い塔を建設することにより利用できる。⁴風が吹いてそのプロペラを回し，プロペラが電気を発生させるように発電機を回転させる。⁵私たちは，「ウィンドファーム（風力発電地帯）」を作ってより多くの電気を発生させるために，このような塔を数多くまとめて建設する傾向がある。⁶塔が多ければ多いほど，風がたくさん吹けば吹くほど，プロペラが大きければ大きいほど，たくさんの電気を作ることができる。⁷強くて一定の風が吹く場所に風力発電地帯を建設しないと価値はない。

Check! 第2文 ... and we feel a wind blowing の feel は知覚動詞の用法。feel O *doing* で「O が～しているのを感じる」の意味。

語句

heat	動	熱する，温める
atmosphere	名	大気
unevenly	副	不均等に，不規則に
warm	形	温かい
rise up	熟	上昇する
blow in	熟	吹き込む
replace	動	取って代わる
propeller	名	プロペラ，推進器
round	副	回って
turn	動	回転させる，回す
generator	名	発電機
produce	動	生産する，生み出す
electricity	名	電気
tend to *do*	熟	～する傾向がある
It is worth *doing*	熟	～するのは価値がある，～するだけのことはある
steady	形	一定の，絶え間ない

第3段落　文の構造と語句のチェック

¹The best places 〔 for wind farms 〕 are (in coastal areas), (at the tops 〔 of rounded hills 〕), (on open plains) and (in gaps 〔 in mountains 〕) — places 〔 where the wind is strong and reliable 〕. ²Some are offshore. ³(To be worthwhile), you need an average wind speed of around 25 km/h. ⁴Most wind farms 〔 in the UK 〕

(S / V① / ② / ③ / 等接 ④ / 関副)
(S / V / C① / 等接② / C / S / V / C / S / V / O / S)

94

are (in Cornwall or Wales). ⁵Isolated places 〔 such as farms 〕 may have
<u>V</u>   ①   等接 ②   <u>S</u>   <u>V</u>

their own wind generators. ⁶Several wind farms supply electricity (to homes
<u>O</u>   <u>S</u>   <u>V</u>   <u>O</u>

〔 around Los Angeles in California 〕).

訳 ¹風力発電地帯を作るのにもっとも適した場所は，沿岸地域や丸みを帯びた丘のてっぺん，開けた平原，山の谷間である。つまり，風が強くて，確実に吹いてくれる場所だ。²風力発電地帯の中には沖合にあるものもある。³発電をするに値するためには，およそ時速25km の平均風速が必要である。⁴イギリスのほとんどの風力発電地帯はコーンウォールまたはウェールズにある。⁵農場のような隔絶した場所には，その場所専用の風力発電装置があるかもしれない。⁶いくつかの風力発電地帯がカリフォルニア州ロサンゼルス周辺の家庭に電力を供給している。

語句

coastal	形	沿岸の	**reliable**	形	確かな，あてになる
rounded	形	丸みを帯びた，曲線的な	offshore	副	沖合に
open	形	広々とした，開けた	**worthwhile**	形	価値がある，役立つ
plain	名	平原，平野	**average**	形	平均の
gap	名	谷間，峡谷，峠	**isolated**	形	孤立した，隔絶した
			supply	動	供給する

第4段落　文の構造と語句のチェック

¹The propellers are large, (to take energy out (from the largest possible
<u>S</u>   <u>V</u>   <u>C</u>   <u>V'</u>   <u>O'</u>

volume of air)). ²The angle of the blades can be changed, (to cope with varying
<u>S</u>   <u>V</u>

wind speeds), and the generator and propeller can turn (to face the wind)
等接   ① 等接 ②   <u>S</u>   <u>V</u>

(wherever it comes from). ³Some designs use vertical turbines, which don't
関副   <u>S</u> <u>V</u>   <u>S</u>   <u>V</u>   <u>O</u>   関代

need to be turned (to face the wind). ⁴The towers are tall, (to get
<u>V</u>   <u>S</u>   <u>V</u> <u>C</u>   <u>V'</u>

the propellers <u>as</u> high <u>as possible</u>, (up to ⟨ <u>where</u> <u>the wind</u> <u>is</u> <u>stronger</u> ⟩)). ⁵<u>This</u>
   O′   関副 S V C   S

<u>means</u> ⟨ <u>that</u> the land beneath <u>can still be used</u> (for farming)⟩.
 V O従接   S   V

訳 ¹可能な限り大きな体積の空気からエネルギーを取り出すために，プロペラは大きくなっている。²ブレードの角度は，変化する風速に対処できるよう，変えられるようになっており，風がどこから吹いてきても，発電機とプロペラはその風の方を向くことができるようになっている。³一部の設計では垂直のタービンが使われており，これは風の方を向くために回転させる必要がない。⁴プロペラを，できるだけ高く，風がより強い場所に届かせるために，塔は高くなっている。⁵このことは，下の土地が依然として農業に利用できることを意味する。

Check! 第3文 Some designs use vertical turbines, which don't need to be turned to face the wind. の which は【非制限用法】の関係代名詞で，vertical turbines が先行詞。

Check! 第4文 ..., up to where the wind is stronger. の up to は「～まで，～に達して」の意味の前置詞句。where は関係副詞で，where の直前に先行詞 the place が省略されている。

語 句

take out ~	熟	～を取り出す
volume	名	体積，容量
angle	名	角度
blade	名	(プロペラなどの)ブレード，羽根，刃
cope with ~	熟	～に対処する
vary	動	変化する，変動する

face	動	面する，向かう
wherever	接	どこに…しても
vertical	形	垂直の
turbine	名	タービン
		(＊回転する原動機)
beneath	副	下に，下の方に
farming	名	農業

文法事項の整理 ⑨　the＋比較級

第2段落第6文の〈the＋比較級〉についてみてみよう。

The more towers, **the more** wind, and **the larger** the propellers, **the more** electricity we can make.

　比較にはさまざまな定型表現がある。〈The＋比較級〜，the＋比較級 ...〉は「〜すればするほど…」という意味。ここで，比較級に the がつく表現を整理しておこう。

■比較級に the がつく定型表現

① **The＋比較級〜，the＋比較級 ...「〜すればするほど…」**

　例　The older we grow, the poorer our memory becomes.
　　　「年を取れば取るほど，記憶力が悪くなる」

② **the＋比較級＋of the two「2者のうちより…なほう」**

　例　My brother is the taller of the two boys.
　　　「私の弟は2人の少年のうち，より背が高いほうです」

③ **(all) the＋比較級＋理由〜「〜のせいでよりいっそう…」**

　例　I like him all the better for his faults.
　　　= I like him all the better because he has faults.
　　　「私は彼に欠点があるからこそ，よりいっそう彼のことが好きだ」

④ **none the＋比較級＋理由〜「〜であるにもかかわらず…ない」**

　例　I like him none the better for his kindness.
　　　= I like him none the better because he is kind.
　　　「私は彼が親切であるにもかかわらず，彼のことが好きでない」

⑤ **none the less＋理由〜「〜であるにもかかわらず…だ」**

　例　I like him none the less for his faults.
　　　= I like him none the less because he has faults.
　　　「私は彼に欠点があるにもかかわらず，彼のことが好きだ」

（第２段落第６文）

The more towers, the more wind, and the larger the propellers, the more electricity we can make.

▶ 〈The＋比較級〜，the＋比較級 ...〉「〜すればするほど…」のパターンだが，前半部分にあたる〈The＋比較級〜〉が A, B, and C の形で３つ並列されている点に注意。また，この構文では SV がなかったり，be 動詞が省略されたりすることも多い。省略を補うと，以下のようになる。

▶ The more towers (there are), the more wind (there is), and the larger the propellers (are), the more electricity we can make.

語句リストの復習

/20点

次の語句の意味をア〜トからそれぞれ１つ選べ。

1 grind	11 average	ア 大気	コ 面する
2 coastal	12 supply	イ 平均の	サ 供給する
3 corn	13 angle	ウ 言葉	シ 穀物
4 replace	14 vertical	エ 取って代わる	ス 熱する
5 term	15 steady	オ 生産する	セ 電気
6 produce	16 atmosphere	カ 角度	ソ 変化する
7 heat	17 electricity	キ 水を引く	タ すりつぶす
8 vary	18 face	ク 一定の，安定した	チ 沿岸の
9 reliable	19 volume		ツ 価値がある
10 worthwhile	20 irrigate	ケ 確かな，信頼できる	テ 垂直の
			ト 体積，容量

答 1―タ　2―チ　3―シ　4―エ　5―ウ　6―オ　7―ス　8―ソ　9―ケ　10―ツ
11―イ　12―サ　13―カ　14―テ　15―ク　16―ア　17―セ　18―コ　19―ト　20―キ

ディクテーションしてみよう！ 🔊 41-44

今回学習した英文に出てきた単語を，音声を聞いて（　　　）に書き取ろう。

We've used the wind as an energy source for a long time. The Babylonians and Chinese were using wind power to pump water for ❶(i　　　　) ❷(c　　　　) 4,000 years ago, and sailing boats were around long before that. Wind power was used in the Middle Ages, in Europe, to grind corn, which is where the ❸(t　　　　) "windmill" comes from.

The sun heats our ❹(a　　　　) unevenly, so some parts become warmer than others. These warm parts rise up, other air blows in to ❺(r　　　　) them — and we feel a wind blowing. We can use the energy in the wind by building a tall tower, with a large propeller on the top. The wind blows the propeller round, which turns a generator to produce electricity. We tend to build many of these towers together, to make a "wind farm" and produce more electricity. The more towers, the more wind, and the larger the propellers, the more electricity we can make. It's only worth building wind farms in places that have strong, ❻(s　　　　) winds.

The best places for wind farms are in coastal areas, at the tops of rounded hills, on open plains and in gaps in mountains — places where the wind is strong and ❼(r　　　　). Some are offshore. To be worthwhile, you need an ❽(a　　　　) wind speed of around 25 km/h. Most wind farms in the UK are in Cornwall or Wales. Isolated places such as farms may have their own wind generators. Several wind farms ❾(s　　　　) electricity to homes around Los Angeles in California.

The propellers are large, to take energy out from the largest possible ❿(v　　　　) of air. The ⓫(a　　　　) of the blades can be changed, to cope with varying wind speeds, and the generator and propeller can turn to face the wind wherever it comes from. Some designs use ⑫(v) turbines, which don't need to be turned to face the wind. The towers are tall, to get the propellers as high as possible, up to where the wind is stronger. This means that the land beneath can still be used for farming.

解 答

問1	（ア） ③	（イ） ①	（ウ） ②	（エ） ②	（オ） ④
	（カ） ③	（キ） ④	（ク） ①	（ケ） ②	（コ） ③
問2	②，⑤，⑨				

解 説

問1

（ア）「とても楽に」 選択肢はそれぞれ，①「とても頻繁に」，②「とても苦労して」，③「とても容易に」，④「ほとんど理由もなく」の意味。

（イ）「～に参加する」 選択肢はそれぞれ，①「～において役割を果たす」，②「創造する」，③「～でうまくやる」，④「教える」の意味。

（ウ）「～を奪われて」 選択肢はそれぞれ，①「～に加えられて」，②「～との接触を与えられずに」，③「～につながって」，④「～から盗まれて」。②の deny は，第3文型(S+V+O)で「Oを否定する」，第4文型(S+V+O₁+O₂)で「O₁にO₂を与えない」の意味。

（エ）「著しく」 選択肢はそれぞれ，①「たいてい」，②「とても」，③「ある程度は」，④「まったく～ない」の意味。

（オ）「苦労して」 選択肢はそれぞれ，①「長い間」，②「無邪気に」，③「さまざまな方法で」，④「おおいに苦労しながら」の意味。

（カ）「…する限り」 選択肢はそれぞれ，①「…する間に」，②「…と同様に」，③「もし…ならば，…という条件で」，④「同様に」。as long as … は「…する限り」の意味だが，while に近い意味で【時】を表す場合（例 as long as I live「生きている限り」）と，【条件】を表す場合（例 as long as you keep quiet「静かにしている限り」）の2つの意味がある。本文では後者の意味。

（キ）「～に触れさせられて」 選択肢はそれぞれ，①「示す」，②「買われる」，③「習得する」，④「～と接触する」。expose A to B は「A(人)をB(考え方，文化など)に触れさせる，体験させる」の意味。ここはその受け身。

（ク）「上手な，熟達した」 選択肢はそれぞれ，①「巧みな，熟練した」，②

「現実的な」，③「おもしろい，愉快な」，④「幸運な」の意味。

(ケ)「影響されて」 選択肢はそれぞれ，①「改良されて」，②「影響されて」，
③「示されて」，④「理解されて」の意味。

(コ)「重大な，決定的な」 選択肢はそれぞれ，①「大きな」，②「開放的な」，
③「重要な」，④「浅い」の意味。

問2

① 「コミュニケーションをするために言語を覚える機会を逃す子供は決して
いない」

▶ 第1段落第2文と不一致。miss out on ～ は「～の機会を逃す」の意味。

②「言語は我々を人間らしくする主たる要素の1つである」

▶ 第1段落第1文の and plays 以降と一致。

③ 「子供たちはいかなる年齢でも問題なく言語学習を始めることができる」

▶ 第1段落最終文，第2段落最終文，第3段落第5，6文と不一致。

④ 「大変な努力の後，ヴィクトールは少々の言葉を話せるようになった」

▶ 第2段落最終文と不一致。

**⑤「イタールはヴィクトールに少し読むことを教えるのには成功したが，話
すことは教えられなかった」**

▶ 第2段落最終文と一致。

⑥ 「耳の聞こえない子供たちは，言語から隔離された子供たちよりも状況が
悪い」

▶ 最終段落第1文と不一致。be worse off（than ～）で「（～よりも）状況が
ひどい，暮らし向きが悪い」の意味。

⑦ 「耳の聞こえない子供や言語から隔離された子供にとっては，語彙よりも
文法を習得する方が容易である」

▶ 最終段落最後の2文と不一致。

⑧ 「手話は耳の聞こえない子供たちにとって無益である」

▶ 最終段落第2文と不一致。

⑨「比較的早い年齢までに文法を学習することが不可欠である」

▶ 最終段落最終文と一致。

それでは次に，段落ごとに詳しくみていこう。　🔊 45

第1段落　文の構造と語句のチェック

Growing up without language

¹It is almost impossible 〈 for us to imagine growing up without language 〉,
(仮S V C 真S S' V')

which develops (in our minds) (so effortlessly) (in early childhood) and plays
(V① 等接 V②)

such a central role (in 〈 defining us as human 〉 and 〈 allowing us to participate
(O ① 等接 ② V' O' C')

in our culture 〉). ²Nevertheless, 〈 being deprived of language 〉 occasionally
(S)

happens. ³(In recent centuries) children have been found living in the wild,
(V S V C)

being 省略

(said to have been raised by wolves or other animals and deprived of human
(① 等接 ②)

contact.) ⁴It is hard 〈 to know the real stories [behind these cases]〉, but they
(仮S V C 真S V' O' 等接 S)

are all strikingly similar (with respect to language). ⁵The pattern is 〈 that
(V C S V C 従接)

the children

only those [rescued early in childhood] developed an ability [to speak]〉.
(S V O)

The children

⁶ Those [found (after they were about nine years old)] learned only a few
(S 従接 S V C V O)

words, or failed to learn language (at all).
(等接 V O)

訳　　　　　　　　　言語なしで成長すること

¹私たちが言語なしで育つことを想像するのはほとんど不可能である。なぜなら言語は，子供時代の初期にとても容易に頭の中で発達するものであるし，私たちを人間と定義する上で，また，私たちが自分たちの文化に参加することを可能にする上で，とても重要な役割を果たしているからだ。²にもかかわらず，言語を奪われるということが時折起こる。³ここ数百年の間に子供たちが野生の状態で生活しているのが発見され，オオカミやその他の動物によって育てられて人間との接触を奪われたと言われている。⁴このような事例の背後にある真相を知ることは困難だが，言語に関してはみな著しく似通っている。⁵幼少期の初期に救われた子供しか言語を話す能力は発達しないというパターンがあるのだ。⁶およそ9歳以降に発見された子供たちは，ごくわずかの言葉しか覚えなかったり，言語を身につけることがまったくできなかったりしたのだ。

Check! 第1文 … and allowing us to participate in our culture の〈allow + O + to do〉は，①「O が～するのを許可する」（= permit），②「O が～するのを可能にする」（= enable）の2つの意味を持つ。原則として，①は S が人間の場合，②は S が物事の場合である。ここでは②の意味。

Check! 第3文 In recent centuries children have been found living in the wild, said to have been raised by wolves or other animals and deprived of human contact. の said は過去分詞で，前に being が省略された分詞構文（【付帯状況】の意味）と考える。have been の後は raised と deprived が並列されている。

語　句

imagine	動	想像する	recent	形	最近の
develop	動	発達する〔させる〕	century	名	世紀，百年
effortlessly	副	苦労せず，楽に	in the wild	熟	野生で，自然界で
childhood	名	子供時代，幼少期	raise	動	育てる
play a role	熟	役割を果たす	wolf	名	オオカミ
central	形	中心的な，主要な			（複数形 wolves）
define A as B	熟	A を B と定義する	contact	名	接触
human	形	人間の	case	名	事例，実例
allow	動	可能にする	strikingly	副	著しく
participate in ~	熟	～に参加する	similar	形	よく似て，類似して
culture	名	文化	with respect to ~	熟	～に関して
nevertheless	副	にもかかわらず，それなのに	pattern	名	パターン，決まった型
			rescue	動	救う，救助する
deprive A of B	熟	A から B を奪う	ability	名	能力
occasionally	副	時折，時々	fail to do	熟	～できない，～しない
			at all	熟	（否定文で）全く，全然

第2段落　文の構造と語句のチェック

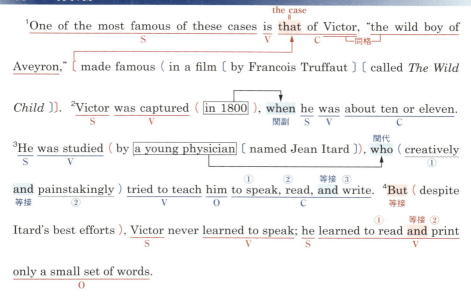

¹One of the most famous of these cases is **that** of Victor, "the wild boy of Aveyron," [made famous (in a film [by Francois Truffaut] [called *The Wild Child*]]. ²Victor was captured (in 1800), when he was about ten or eleven. ³He was studied (by a young physician [named Jean Itard]), who (creatively and painstakingly) tried to teach him to speak, read, and write. ⁴But (despite Itard's best efforts), Victor never learned to speak; he learned to read and print only a small set of words.

> 訳 ¹このような事例のもっとも有名なものの1つが，フランソワ・トリュフォー監督による映画 The Wild Child で有名になった「アヴェロンの野生児」，ヴィクトールの事例である。²ヴィクトールは1800年に捕らえられ，その頃10歳か11歳ぐらいだった。³彼はジャン・イタールという名の若い医師により研究され，ジャン・イタールは独創的なやり方で辛抱強く，彼に話すこと，読むこと，書くことを教えようとした。⁴しかしイタールの精一杯の努力にもかかわらず，ヴィクトールはまったく話せるようにならなかった。彼はわずかな一連の単語のみ，読んだり活字体で書いたりできるようになっただけであった。

Check! 第1文 One of the most famous of these cases is that of Victor, "the wild boy of Aveyron," made famous in a film by François Truffaut called *The Wild Child.* の代名詞 that は the case の代用。また，Victor と "the wild boy of Aveyron" が同格。made は第5文型で「OをCにする」の意味。ここでは that of Victor を修飾する過去分詞。

第3段落　文の構造と語句のチェック

as children without language 省略

¹Children〔without hearing〕are not as handicapped. ²A deaf child can still
S　　　　　　　　　　　　　　　V　　C　　　　　　　S

have language and relate normally (to others)(through signing)—(as long as
V①　　O　　等接　V②　　　　　　　　　　　　　　　　　　　　従接

language development starts early). ³There are a number of studies〔that
S　　　　　　　　V　　　　　　　　　　V　　　S　　　　　関代

show〈that (the sooner a deaf child is exposed (to a natural sign language),
V　　O従接　　　　　　　S　　　　V

〔such as American Sign Language 〕), the more proficient a signer he or she
C　　　　　　　S

will become〉]. ⁴(As in other cases of linguistic isolation), the ability〔of deaf
V　　　　　従接　　　　　　　　　　　　　　　　　　　　　S

people 〕〔 to learn new *words* 〕is not affected (by the age 〔at which they
V　　　　　　　　　　　　　関代　S

are exposed (to language)]). ⁵But their ability〔 to learn grammar 〕is
V　　　　　　　　　　等接　S

dramatically affected. ⁶Studies〔 of deaf children 〔 exposed to sign language
V　　　　S

(after the preschool years)]] show 〈 that there is a critical period〔 for
V　O従接　　V　　S

grammatical development 〕, which ends, perhaps, (in the early school-age
関代　　　　　V

years)〉.

訳 ¹聴覚を持たない子供たちは，それに比べると不利ではない。²耳の聞こえない子供は，それでも言語を持ち，手話を通じて他者との関係を正常に結ぶことができる——言語の発達が早期に始まっている限りは。³耳の聞こえない子供が，アメリカ手話のような自然な手話に早く触れれば触れるほど，上手に手話を使えるようになる，ということを示す多数の研究がある。⁴言語的隔離の他の事例と同様に，耳の聞こえない人々が新しい言葉を覚える能力は言語に触れる年齢によっては影響されない。⁵しかし，文法を覚える能力は劇的に影響を受ける。⁶就学前の幼児期を過ぎてから手話に触れた，耳の聞こえない子供たちに関する研究が示すところによれば，文法的発達には臨界期が存在し，文法力の発達はおそらく，就学年齢に達してからの数年で終わってしまうというのだ。

Check! 第 1 文 Children without hearing are not as handicapped. では，〈not as [so] ＋ 原級 ＋ as 〜〉「〜ほど…ない」の後ろの as 〜 が省略されている。省略を補うなら，as children without language，または直前の段落に比較対照があると考え，as Victor となろう。

Check! 第 3 文 There are a number of studies that show that the sooner a deaf child is exposed to a natural sign language, such as American Sign Language, the more proficient a signer he or she will become. では，〈The ＋ 比較級〜，the 比較級 ...〉「〜すればするほど…」がポイント（→ p. 97 参照）。

語句

hearing	名	聴力，聴覚		sign language	名	手話
handicapped	形	障害のある，不利な立場にある		such as 〜	熟	〜のような
				proficient	形	上手な，熟達した
deaf	形	耳が聞こえない		signer	名	手話を使う人，手話通訳者
relate to 〜	熟	〜(人)と良い関係を結ぶ，うまく付き合う		linguistic	形	言語(学)の
				isolation	名	孤立，分断，隔離
normally	副	普通に，正常に		affect	動	影響する
sign	動	手話を用いる		grammar	名	文法
as long as ...	熟	…する限り		dramatically	副	劇的に
development	名	発達		preschool	形	就学前の
a number of 〜	熟	多数の〜		critical	形	重大な，決定的な
study	名	研究，調査		▶ critical period	名	臨界期
expose A to B	熟	A を B にさらす，触れさせる				(＊発達過程において，その時期を過ぎるとある行動の学習が成立しなくなる限界の時期)
natural	形	自然な		grammatical	形	文法の，文法的な
				school-age	形	学齢期の

107

文法事項の整理 ⑩　「…する限り」

第３段落第２文の as long as についてみてみよう。

... **as long as** language development starts early

■「…する限り」の意味をもつ接続詞

「…する限り」の意味を表す接続詞には，以下の２つがある。

1）**as [so] far as ...**	▶【範囲】を表す。
2）**as [so] long as ...**	▶【時間】【条件】を表す。

　このうち，2)の【時間】は while に，【条件】は if only に意味が近い。したがって，while や if only に置き換えられる場合は as [so] long as ...，どちらとも置き換えられない場合は as [so] far as ... と考えるとよい。
　練習してみよう。

間　次の各英文の（　　）に far か long を入れよ。

1）I won't let him have his own way as （　　） as I live.

2）As （　　） as I am concerned, I have no objection to the idea.

3）You can stay in this room, as （　　） as you keep quiet.

4）As （　　） as the eye could reach, nothing was to be seen but snow.

5）As （　　） as I know, he is an honest man.

6）Anything will do as （　　） as it is interesting.

解答

1）**long**「私が生きている限り（＝生きている間），彼に好き勝手なことはさせない」

　▶ while に近い。【時間】を表す。

2）**far**「私に関する限り，その見解に対する反論はない」

　▶ while や if only とは置き換えられない。【範囲】を表す。なお，as [so] far as S is concerned「S に関する限り」は決まり文句として覚

えよう。

3) **long**「君は静かにしている限り，この部屋にいてよろしい」
   ▶ if only に近い。【条件】を表す。

4) **far**「目が届く限り（＝目が届く範囲内では），雪以外に何も見えなかった」
   ▶【範囲】を表す。

5) **far**「私の知る限り（＝私が知っている範囲内では），彼は正直者だ」
   ▶【範囲】を表す。なお，as [so] far as S know「S が知る限り」（＝ to the best of S's knowledge）も決まり文句として覚えよう。

6) **long**「興味深いものである限り，何でもかまわない」
   ▶ if only に近い。【条件】を表す。

語句リストの復習

次の語句の意味を**ア**〜**ト**からそれぞれ１つ選べ。

/20点

1 develop	11 creatively
2 fail to *do*	12 try to *do*
3 childhood	13 deaf
4 raise	14 isolation
5 define *A* as *B*	15 ability
6 strikingly	16 recent
7 deprive *A* of *B*	17 with respect
8 expose *A* to *B*	to 〜
9 capture	18 linguistic
10 physician	19 despite
	20 imagine

ア 〜しようとする	サ 〜にもかかわらず
イ 捕まえる	
ウ A を B と定義する	シ 言語(学)の
エ A を B にさらす	ス 耳が聞こえない
オ 〜できない	セ 著しく
カ 想像する	ソ 能力
キ 独創的に	タ 〜に関して
ク 子供時代	チ 育てる
ケ A から B を奪う	ツ 最近の
コ 医師	テ 発達する
	ト 隔離，孤立

答 1—テ 2—オ 3—ク 4—チ 5—ウ 6—セ 7—ケ 8—エ 9—イ 10—コ
11—キ 12—ア 13—ス 14—ト 15—ソ 16—ツ 17—タ 18—シ 19—サ 20—カ

ディクテーションしてみよう！ 🔊 46-48

今回学習した英文に出てきた単語を，音声を聞いて（　　　　）に書き取ろう。

It is almost impossible for us to ❶(i　　　　　) growing up without language, which develops in our minds so effortlessly in early ❷(c　　　　　) and plays such a central role in defining us as human and allowing us to participate in our culture. Nevertheless, being deprived of language occasionally happens. In ❸(r　　　　) centuries children have been found living in the wild, said to have been raised by wolves or other animals and deprived of human contact. It is hard to know the real stories behind these cases, but they are all strikingly similar with ❹(r　　　　) to language.   The pattern is that only those rescued early in childhood developed an ability to speak. Those found after they were about nine years old learned only a few words, or ❺(f　　　　) to learn language at all.

One of the most famous of these cases is that of Victor, "the wild boy of Aveyron," made famous in a film by François Truffaut called *The Wild Child*. Victor was ❻(c　　　　) in 1800, when he was about ten or eleven. He was studied by a young ❼(p　　　　) named Jean Itard, who creatively and painstakingly tried to teach him to speak, read, and write. But ❽(d　　　　) Itard's best efforts, Victor never learned to speak; he learned to read and print only a small set of words.

Children without hearing are not as handicapped. A ❾(d　　　　) child can still have language and relate normally to others through signing — as long as language development starts early.   There are a number of studies that show that the sooner a deaf child is ❿(e　　　　) to a natural sign language, such as American

110

Sign Language, the more proficient a signer he or she will become. As in other cases of ⑪(1) isolation, the ability of deaf people to learn new *words* is not affected by the age at which they are exposed to language. But their ability to learn grammar is dramatically affected. Studies of deaf children exposed to sign language after the preschool years show that there is a critical period for grammatical development, which ends, perhaps, in the early school-age years.

答 ❶ imagine ❷ childhood ❸ recent ❹ respect ❺ failed ❻ captured ❼ physician ❽ despite ❾ deaf ❿ exposed ⑪ linguistic

11 解答・解説

解答

問1 ④	問2 ④	問3 ②	問4 ④
問5 ②	問6 ④	問7 ②, ③	

解説

問1

① 「ガスがないため，まったく爆発の起こらない恒星もある」

▶ 第1段落第2，3文と不一致。

② 「恒星は通常，表面上で 1,000 以下の爆発が起きる」

▶ 第1段落第3文と不一致。

③ 「恒星の色は周囲で起こる爆発と関係がない」

▶ 第1段落最終文と不一致。

④ **「恒星の熱や光は，星の表面上での爆発によって生じる」**

▶ 第1段落第4文と一致。

問2

① 「太陽と比較して，オレンジ色に見える恒星はずっと高温である」

▶ 第2段落最終文と不一致。

② 「恒星は太陽よりも低温だと青色に見える場合がある」

▶ 第2段落第6文と不一致。

③ 「燃焼して太陽よりもずっと高温になる恒星は存在しない」

▶ 第2段落第5文後半と不一致。

④ **「太陽よりも多くのエネルギーを生み出す恒星もある」**

▶ 第2段落第5文前半と一致。

問3

　まず，下線部の turn into ～ は「～に変化する」という意味なので，③と④は消去できる。次に，下線部後半（主節）は，「太陽の外側が木星の軌道を越えるだろう」とあるが，これは太陽が超巨星になった場合の大きさの説明であり，木星の軌道がすっぽり入ってしまうほどであることを比喩的に述べている。以

上により，②が正解とわかる。各選択肢の意味は以下のとおり。

① 「もし太陽が赤色の超巨星になったら，木星は太陽から遠く離れるであろう」

② **「もし太陽が赤色の超巨星に変化したら，木星は太陽の中に入ってしまうであろう」**

③ 「もし太陽が赤色の超巨星に衝突したら，木星はもはや存在しなくなってしまうであろう」

④ 「もし太陽が赤色の超巨星の周りを回ったら，太陽は木星に接近するであろう」

問4

① 「矮星は太陽と同じ大きさになることはあり得ない」
▶ 第3段落第2文と不一致。太陽も矮星（dwarf）である。

② 「宇宙で最大の星の1つが太陽である」
▶ 第3段落第2文後半と不一致。もっと大きい恒星が数多く存在する，とある。

③ 「赤色の超巨星は矮星の一種である」
▶ 第3段落第4文と不一致。赤色の超巨星は最大の恒星であり，他方，矮星とは小さな恒星のこと（第2段落第3文参照）である。

④ **「さまざまな大きさの星が存在する」**
▶ 第3段落第1文と一致。

問5

　下線部の2つのit は，いずれも太陽（the sun）を指す。主節で It will not become a supergiant「超巨星にはならない」とあり，従属節ではその理由として，because it is not heavy enough「十分な重さがないから」とある。よって，②が正解。各選択肢の意味は以下のとおり。

① 「太陽は，重くなるにつれて，ゆっくりと超巨星へと発達するであろう」
② **「重量のせいで，太陽は超巨星になる可能性はない」**
③ 「太陽は重いので，超巨星と同じ大きさになり得る」
④ 「太陽は十分に重量を減らした時，超巨星になるであろう」

問6

① 「太陽は赤色の巨星になった後，急速に冷たく暗くなる」

▶ 最終段落第3，5文および最終文と不一致。巨星になった後，まず高温になってから，ゆっくりと冷たく暗くなるのである。

② 「地球上の生物は太陽が赤色の巨星になった後も生き残るであろう」

▶ 最終段落第6文と不一致。

③ 「太陽はその寿命を終えた後も光と熱を生み出し続ける」

▶ 最終段落最終文と不一致。

④ **「太陽がその寿命を終えると，地球の気温はずっと高温になるであろう」**

▶ 最終段落第5，6文と一致。

問7

① 「地球が太陽から受けるエネルギーの形態は熱と光である」

▶ 第2段落第2文と一致。

② **「地球は主として赤色の超巨星によって生み出されるエネルギーによってあたためられている」**

▶ そのような記述はない。また，地球に熱を送る太陽は超巨星ではない（第2段落第3文）。

③ **「太陽は『黄色矮星』と呼ばれる他のすべての恒星よりもずっと大きい」**

▶ 第2段落第3文によれば，太陽自体が黄色矮星の1つなのであり，太陽が他の黄色矮星より大きいという記述はない。

④ 「白色の恒星と赤色の恒星の温度は同じではない」

▶ 第2段落第6，7文と一致。

⑤ 「宇宙空間の多くの恒星は太陽の100倍以上の大きさである」

▶ 第3段落第3文と一致。

⑥ 「太陽はこの先何百万年も存在し続けると予想されている」

▶ 最終段落第2文と一致。

⑦ 「太陽は巨星にはなり得るが超巨星にはなり得ない」

▶ 最終段落第3，4文と一致。

それでは次に，段落ごとに詳しくみていこう。 49

第1段落　文の構造と語句のチェック

¹A star is a big ball of fire〔in space〕〔that makes lots of light and other forms
　　　S　 V　　　 C　　　　　　　　 関代　　V　　　　　　①　　等接②　　O

of energy〕. ²A star is mostly made up（of gases and something like fire,〔only
　　　　　　　　　 S　　　　　 V　　　　　　①　 等接　　　　②

much hotter〕）. ³There are thousands of explosions happening（all over the
　　　　　　V　　　　　　　 S

star）（all the time）. ⁴This is〈where the star's heat and light come from〉.
　　　　　　　　　　　　 S　 V C 関副　　　①　　等接②　　　　V
　　　　　　　　　　　　　　　　　　　　　　　S

⁵These explosions are also〈where a star gets its color from〉.
　　　 S　　　　 V　　　 C 関副　 S　　V　　O

訳 ¹恒星とは多量の光や他の種類のエネルギーを発する，宇宙空間に浮かぶ大きな火の玉のことである。²恒星は主として，ガスや，火のような，ただ火よりもはるかに熱い物により構成されている。³常に恒星のいたるところで，何千もの爆発が起きている。⁴これが，恒星の熱や光が生じる源である。⁵これらの爆発はまた，恒星が色を得る源でもある。

Check! 第3文 There are thousands of explosions happening all over the star all the time. の There is [are] S *doing* は，S is [are] *doing*（進行形）とほぼ同じ内容。したがって，Thousands of explosions are happening all over the star all the time. と同様の意味を表すと考えてよい。なお，There is [are] S *done* は，S is [are] *done*（受動態）とほぼ同じ内容になる。

語句

star	名	恒星，星
space	名	宇宙（空間）
light	名	光
form	名	形態，種類
energy	名	エネルギー
mostly	副	主として，大部分は
be made up of ~	熟	~から成る，~で構成される

gas	名	気体，ガス
thousands of ~	熟	何千もの~
explosion	名	爆発
all over ~	熟	~のいたるところで
all the time	熟	いつも，ずっと
heat	名	熱
color	名	色

¹Our sun is a star. ²It is the closest star 〔 to our planet 〕, and it sends its
　　S　　V　C　　　　S　V　　　　C　　　　　　　　　　　　　　等接　S　V　　O

energy（ to the Earth ）（ as heat and light ）. ³The sun seems large（ to us ）, but
　O　　　　　　　　　　　　①　等接　②　　　　　S　　V　　C　　　　　　　等接

it is only a medium sized star 〔 called a yellow dwarf (small star) 〕. ⁴Other
S　V　　　　　C　　　　　　　　　　　　　　　　　　　　　　　　　　　　　　　　　

stars can be different colors. ⁵Some stars have more energy（ than our sun ）and
　S　　　V　　　　C　　　　　　　S　　V①　　O　　　　　　　　　　　　　　等接

burn even hotter（ than our sun does ）. ⁶Stars 〔 that are hotter（ than our sun ）〕
V②　　　C　　　　　　　　　　　　　　　　　S　　関代　V　　C

may look blue or white. ⁷Stars 〔 that are cooler（ than our sun ）〕 may look
　V　　　　C　　　　　　　S　　関代　V　　C　　　　　　　　　　　　　V

orange or red.
　　C

> 訳 ¹私たちの太陽は恒星である。²それは，私たちの惑星にもっとも近い恒星であり，熱や光としてエネルギーを地球に送っている。³太陽は私たちにとっては大きく思われるが，黄色矮星(小さな恒星)と呼ばれる中型の恒星であるに過ぎない。⁴他の恒星はさまざまな色の場合がある。⁵私たちの太陽よりも大きなエネルギーを持ち，燃焼して太陽よりさらに高温になる恒星もある。⁶私たちの太陽よりも高温の恒星は，青色や白色に見える場合がある。⁷私たちの太陽よりも低温の恒星は，オレンジ色または赤色に見える場合がある。

Check! 第5文 Some stars have more energy than our sun and burn even hotter than our sun does. の〈even [still] ＋比較級〉は「さらに，それ以上に」の意味で，even [still] は**比較級を強調する**。これは，程度が高いものと比較して，さらにそれを上回るという意味である。なお，第1段落第2文や第3段落第2文，最終段落第1文にある〈much [a lot / far] ＋比較級〉は「ずっと，はるかに」の意味で，差が大きいことを表す。

語句

close 形 近い	medium-sized 形 (大きさが)中くらいの
▶活用：close-closer-closest	dwarf 名 矮星
planet 名 惑星，地球	burn 動 燃えて〜になる
	cool 形 涼しい，冷えた

116

第3段落　文の構造と語句のチェック

¹Stars come (in many sizes).　²Our sun is about 1.4 million kilometers
　S　　V　　　　　　　　　　　　　　　S　　V　　　　　　　　C

around, but people still call it a dwarf (because many stars are much bigger).
　　　　等接　S　　　　V　O　　C　　　　従接　　　S　　　V　　　C

³(For example), there are many stars 〔 which are more than 100 times bigger
　　　　　　　　　　　　V　　S　　　　　関代　V　　　　　　　C

(than our sun)〕.　⁴The largest stars are called red supergiants.　⁵These stars
　　　　　　　　　　　　S　　　　　V　　　C　　　　　S

are so big (that most of our small solar system would fit (inside one)).　⁶(If our
　V　C　　従接　　　　　　　S　　　　　　　　V　　　　　　　　　　　　従接

sun turned (into a red supergiant)), the outside of the sun would be (past
　S　V　　　　　　　　　　　　　　　　　　　　S　　　　　　　　　V

Jupiter's orbit).

訳 ¹恒星には多くの大きさのものがある。²私たちの太陽は周囲がおよそ 140 万 km あるが、それでも人々は太陽を矮星と呼ぶ。なぜなら、多くの恒星が太陽よりもはるかに大きいからだ。³たとえば、太陽の 100 倍以上の大きさの恒星が数多く存在するのだ。⁴最も大きな恒星は赤色超巨星と呼ばれる。⁵こういった恒星は非常に大きいので、私たちの小さな太陽系のほとんどが、その恒星の中に入ってしまうほどだ。⁶もし私たちの太陽が赤色超巨星に変化するとしたら、太陽の外周は木星の軌道を越えてしまうであろう。

Check!　第5文 These stars are so big that most of our small solar system would fit inside one. は〈so ～ that …〉構文「とても～なので…」になっており、that 以下で助動詞 would が使われているのは、仮定法の意味を表すため。実際に太陽系が恒星の中に入るわけではないが、大きさの面ですっぽり入ってしまうほどである、という内容。文末の one は one of these stars と考えればよい。

語句

come in ～	熟	～の種類〔形式〕がある	million	形 百万の
size	名 大きさ		kilometer	名 キロメートル
			around	副 周囲で、一周すると

still	副	それでも（なお）	**outside**	名	外側
supergiant	名	超巨星	**past**	前	〜を過ぎて，〜を越えて
solar system	名	太陽系	Jupiter	名	木星
inside	前	〜の中に，〜の内側に	**orbit**	名	軌道
turn into 〜	熟	〜に変わる，〜に変化する			

第4段落　文の構造と語句のチェック

¹Stars, (just like people), have a life, but a star's life is much longer (than a
S 　　　　　　　　　　　　 V 　O 　等接 　　　S 　　　V 　　C

human's life). ²The sun is millions of years old and will live (for many more
S 　V① 　　　C 　　　　等接 　V②

millions of years). ³(When our sun starts to die), it will grow (into a red giant
従接 　S 　　V 　　　S 　will grow

star). ⁴It will not become a supergiant (because it is not heavy enough).
S 　V 　　　　C 　　　従接 　S 　V 　　C

⁵(When our sun dies), it will get so hot (that the heat and light will burn the
従接 　S 　V 　　　S 　V 　C 　　従接 　　①　　等接②　S 　　　　V

Earth). ⁶(In fact), it will be too hot (for anything to live (on the Earth))
O 　　　　　　　 S 　V 　C 　　S' 　　　V'

(when our sun becomes a red giant). ⁷Then, our sun will slowly get darker and
従接 　S 　V 　　　C 　　　　　　S 　　　V 　　　C

colder (until it stops 〈 giving off any energy 〉 (at all)).
従接 S 　V 　O

> **訳** ¹恒星には人間とちょうど同じように，寿命がある。だが，恒星の寿命は人間の寿命よりずっと長い。²太陽はできてから何百万年もたっており，これからもさらに何百万年も存続するだろう。³太陽が終わりを迎えようとすると，赤色巨星へと変化を遂げるであろう。⁴太陽は超巨星にはならない。なぜなら，十分な重量がないからだ。⁵太陽が死ぬとき，非常に熱くなるので，その熱と光で地球は燃やされてしまうであろう。⁶実際，太陽が赤色巨星になると，あまりに熱くなるため，いかなるものも地球上で生きられなくなるであろう。⁷その後，太陽はゆっくりと暗く，冷たくなり，ついにはまったく熱を発しなくなるだろう。

🌀 Check! 最終段落最終文の until の意味のとり方に注意しよう。基本的に，接続詞 until [till] は，「…するまで」の意味であるが，until [till] の導く節が主節より後に置かれるとき，「ついに…」という意味で理解するとわかりやすい場合がある。例えば，「疲れるまで働き続けた」と「働き続けてついに疲れてしまった」は同様の意味である。本文も，「まったく熱を発しなくなるまでゆっくりと暗く冷たくなってゆく」ととらえてもよいが，「ゆっくりと暗く冷たくなってゆき，ついにはまったく熱を発しなくなる」と理解したほうがわかりやすい。

語 句

life	名	寿命
millions of ~	熟	何百万もの~
grow into ~	熟	~へと成長[発達]する
giant	形	巨大な
	名	巨大なもの
burn	動	燃やす，燃焼する
slowly	副	ゆっくりと
until	接	~するまで，ついに~
stop doing	熟	~するのをやめる，~しなくなる
give off ~	熟	~を発する，放つ
at all	熟	まったく

文法事項の整理 ⑪　仮定法の基本パターン

第３段落最終文をみてみよう。

If our sun **turned** into a red supergiant, the outside of the sun **would be** past Jupiter's orbit.

■仮定法の形

事実に反することを仮定する表現方法を【仮定法】という。これに対し，事実をそのまま述べるのは【直説法】という。

仮定法の特徴は，現在の内容が過去形，過去の内容が過去完了形で書かれる，つまり，いつもとは時制が１つ前にずれるという点である。

① 例　If I were rich, I could buy the house.
「(今)私が金持ちなら，(今)その家を買えるのだが」
→現実は，金持ちでないから買えない。
(≒ As I am not rich, I can't buy the house.)

② 例 If I had been rich, I could have bought the house.

「(あのとき)私が金持ちだったら, (あのとき)その家を買えたのだが」

→現実は, 金持ちでなかったから買えなかった。

(≒ As I was not rich, I couldn't buy the house.)

③ 例 If I had worked hard, I could buy the house.

「(あのとき)熱心に働いていたら, (今)その家を買えるのだが」

→現実は, 熱心に働かなかったから買えない。

(≒ As I did not work hard, I can't buy the house.)

パターンを整理すると以下のようになる。

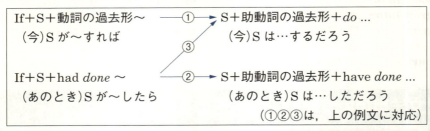

①のパターンを【仮定法過去】, ②のパターンを【仮定法過去完了】という。③は①+②の混合である。

(第3段落最終文)

If our sun turned into a red supergiant, the outside of the sun would be past Jupiter's orbit.

▶ ①のパターン(仮定法過去)になっている。

語句リストの復習

次の語句の意味を**ア〜ト**からそれぞれ1つ選べ。

/20点

1	form	11	solar system
2	planet	12	inside
3	energy	13	past
4	explosion	14	give off 〜
5	mostly	15	close
6	all the time	16	thousands of 〜
7	be made up of 〜	17	heat
8	orbit	18	millions of 〜
9	cool	19	turn into 〜
10	size	20	light

ア	主として	サ	何千もの〜
イ	〜の中に	シ	エネルギー
ウ	涼しい	ス	何百万もの〜
エ	熱	セ	近い
オ	軌道	ソ	光
カ	形態	タ	太陽系
キ	大きさ	チ	惑星
ク	〜に変わる	ツ	いつも
ケ	〜を発する	テ	爆発
コ	〜を超えて	ト	〜から成る

答 1-カ 2-チ 3-シ 4-テ 5-ア 6-ツ 7-ト 8-オ 9-ウ 10-キ
11-タ 12-イ 13-コ 14-ケ 15-セ 16-サ 17-エ 18-ス 19-ク 20-ソ

ディクテーションしてみよう！ 50-53

今回学習した英文に出てきた単語を，音声を聞いて（　　　）に書き取ろう。

　　A star is a big ball of fire in space that makes lots of light and other forms of ❶(e　　　　　). A star is ❷(m　　　　　) made up of gases and something like fire, only much hotter.　There are thousands of explosions happening all over the star all the time.　This is where the star's heat and light come from.　These ❸(e　　　　　　) are also where a star gets its color from.

　　Our sun is a star.　It is the ❹(c　　　　　) star to our ❺(p　　　　), and it sends its energy to the Earth as heat and light.　The sun seems large to us, but it is only a medium-sized star called a yellow dwarf (small star). Other stars can be different colors. Some stars have more energy than our sun and burn even hotter than our sun does. Stars that are hotter than our sun may look blue or white. Stars that are **❻**(c   ) than our sun may look orange or red.

    Stars come in many sizes. Our sun is about 1.4 million kilometers around, but people still call it a dwarf because many stars are much bigger. For example, there are many stars which are more than 100 times bigger than our sun. The largest stars are called red supergiants. These stars are so big that most of our small **❼**(s   ) **❽**(s   ) would fit inside one. If our sun **❾**(t   ) into a red supergiant, the outside of the sun would be past Jupiter's orbit.

    Stars, just like people, have a life, but a star's life is much longer than a human's life. The sun is **❿**(m   ) of years old and will live for many more millions of years. When our sun starts to die, it will grow into a red giant star. It will not become a supergiant because it is not heavy enough. When our sun dies, it will get so hot that the heat and light will burn the Earth. In fact, it will be too hot for anything to live on the Earth when our sun becomes a red giant. Then, our sun will slowly get darker and colder until it stops **⓫**(g   ) off any energy at all.

答 ❶ energy ❷ mostly ❸ explosions ❹ closest ❺ planet ❻ cooler ❼ solar
❽ system ❾ turned ❿ millions ⓫ giving

MEMO

MEMO

MEMO

MEMO

出典一覧：
英文 1：*50 FACTS THAT SHOULD CHANGE THE WORLD* by Jessica Williams, Copyright ©2007 Jessica Williams, Permission from Icon Books Ltd. arranged through The English Agency (Japan) Ltd.　英文 2：From *Master the Catholic High School Entrance Exams 2011* by Peterson's. Copyright 2010. Reprinted with permission of Peterson's, LLC. 英文 3：From Ackert/Lee. *Thoughts & Notions*, 2E. ©2005 Heinle/ELT, a part of Cengage, Inc. Reproduced by permission. www.cengage.com/permissions　英文 4：From *Malarcher. Reading Advantage 2*, 2E. ©2004 Heinle/ELT, a part of Cengage, Inc. Reproduced by permission. www.cengage.com/permissions　英文 5：九州国際大学　英文 6：From *The Five Things We Cannot Change, by David Richo*, ©2005 by David Richo. Reprinted by arrangement with The Permissions Company, LLC on behalf of Shambhala Publications Inc., Boulder, CO www.shambhala.com.　英文 7：From Ackert/Lee. *Thoughts & Notions*, 2E. ©2005 Heinle/ELT, a part of Cengage, Inc. Reproduced by permission. www.cengage.com/permissions 英文 8：Excerpt from pp. 77-8 [350words] from AMERICA'S WOMEN by GAIL COLLINS. COPYRIGHT ©2003 BY GAIL COLLINS. Reprinted by permission of HarperCollins Publishers.　英文 9：From *Wind Power* by Andy Darvill. Reprinted with permission by Andy Darvill　英文 10：From *What happens if you are raised without language?* by Susan Curtiss. Reprinted by permission of Equinox Publishing Ltd.　英文 11：From *Reading for speed and fluency 4* by Casey Malarcher, Paul Nation, Garrett Byrne©2007. Reprinted by permission of Compass Publishing.

大学入試　全レベル問題集　英語長文
レベル３ ［改訂版］ 別冊（問題編）

目 次

編集部より

問題を解くときには英文音声は必要ありませんが，復習の際にはぜひ音声を利用して英文の通し聞きを繰り返しおこなってください。語彙やイントネーションの定着に，音声を介したインプットは非常に効果的です。

次の英文を読んで，あとの問いに答えなさい。

It's only in very recent history that we've been able to dream of living long, active lives. During the Roman Empire, life span was just 22 years. By the Middle Ages in England, some 1,500 years later, there was only a little improvement — people could expect to live about 33 years, and not necessarily healthy years either. The threat of famine was ever-present, and medicine was limited to a few brutal surgical techniques. Plagues often occurred, and the Black Death, which swept through Europe between 1347 and 1351, killed a quarter of the population.

The dramatic improvement in human life span didn't start until the Industrial Revolution, which began in England in the 19th century and spread quickly throughout Europe. Since 1840, the average life span in the longest-lived countries has improved steadily — rising by three months every year. And that growth continues to this day.

問 本文の内容にそくした最も適切なものを①〜④より 1 つ選びなさい。

（ア） From the era of the Roman Empire to the Middle Ages

　① there was a great improvement in life span.

　② there was only a slight improvement in life span.

　③ there was no improvement in life span.

　④ there was a slight decline in life span.

（イ） In the Middle Ages
 ① the Black Death killed one fourth of the population.
 ② medicine cured many people of dreadful diseases.
 ③ fatal disease reduced Europe's population by half.
 ④ famine rarely occurred.

（ウ） The Industrial Revolution
 ① was the chief cause of the Black Death.
 ② caused a sharp decrease in the population of England.
 ③ started after the human life span had improved dramatically.
 ④ was followed by the steady improvement of life span.

（エ） The average life span
 ① has stopped improving in Europe in recent centuries.
 ② has not changed in the longest-lived countries since the 19th century.
 ③ has been falling by three months every year in Europe.
 ④ has been rising by three months every year in the longest-lived countries.

（オ） The title of this passage could be:
 ① The Life of the Middle Ages.
 ② The Industrial Revolution and the Population.
 ③ The Improvement of the Life Span.
 ④ Disease and Life Span.

次の英文を読んで，あとの問いに答えなさい。

　　A vast stretch of land lies untouched by civilization in the back country of the eastern portion of the African continent. （　ア　） the occasional exception of a big-animal hunter, foreigners never enter this area. Aside from the Wandorobo* tribe, even the natives stay away from this particular area because it is the home of the deadly tsetse fly*. The tribe depend on the forest for their lives, eating its roots and fruits and making their homes （　イ　） they find themselves at the end of the day. One of the things they usually eat is honey. They obtain it through an ancient, symbiotic* relationship with a bird known as the Indicator. The scientific community finally confirmed the report that this bird intentionally led the natives to trees containing the honey of wild bees. Other species of honey guides are also known to take advantage of the search efforts of some animals in much the same way （　ウ　） the Indicator uses men.

　　This amazing bird settles in a tree near a Wandorobo camp and sings incessantly* until the men answer it with whistles. It then begins its leading flight. Singing, it hops from tree to tree, （　エ　） the men continue their musical answering call. When the bird reaches the tree, its voice becomes shriller* and its followers examine the tree carefully. The Indicator usually sits just over the bees' nests, and the men hear the sounds of the bees in the hollow trunk*. （　オ　） fire, they smoke most of the bees out of the tree, but those that escape the effects of the smoke attack the men violently. In spite of the attack, the Wandorobos gather the honey and leave a small gift for their bird guide.

＊Wandorobo：ワンドロボ族(ケニアやタンザニアの高地に住む狩猟採集部族)

tsetse fly：ツェツェバエ(アフリカ産のイエバエの一種)

symbiotic：共生の

incessantly：絶え間なく，間断なく

shrill(er)：(より)鋭い

hollow trunk：内部が空になっている木の幹

問 空所(ア)～(オ)に入る最も適切なものをそれぞれ①～④の中から1つ選びなさい。

(ア)　① At　　　② With　　　③ For　　　④ Of

(イ)　① wherever　② however　　③ whenever　④ whoever

(ウ)　① as　　　② which　　　③ but　　　④ who

(エ)　① for　　　② that　　　③ unless　　④ while

(オ)　① Use　　　② To use　　③ Using　　④ Used

次の英文を読んで，あとの問いに答えなさい。

Why would someone decide to stop eating? We know that the body needs food in order to function well. However, many people (ア)fast at some time during their lives. Why is this?

Some people fast for political reasons. In the early 20th century, women in England and the United States weren't allowed to vote. In (**イ**), many women went on fasts. They hoped that fasting would bring attention to (ウ)this injustice. Mohandas Gandhi, the famous Indian leader, fasted 17 times during his life. For Gandhi, fasting was a powerful political tool. In 1943, he fasted to bring attention to his country's need for independence. For 21 days, he went without food. Another famous faster was Cesar Chavez. In the 1960s, he fasted for three weeks. Why? His goal was to bring attention to the terrible working conditions of farm workers in the United States.

Fasting is also a spiritual practice in many religions. Every year during the month of Ramadan, which is a religious holiday, Muslims fast from sunrise to sunset. Many Hindus fast on special occasions, (エ)as do some Christians and Buddhists.

Of course, not everyone fasts for political or religious reasons. Some people occasionally fast just because it makes them feel better. The American writer Mark Twain thought fasting was the best (**オ**) for common illnesses. Whenever he had a cold or a fever, he stopped eating completely. He said that this always made his cold or fever go away. Another American writer, Upton Sinclair, discovered fasting after years of overeating, stomach problems, and headaches. His first fast lasted for 12 days. During this time, his headaches and stomachaches went away. Sinclair said that fasting also made him more alert and energetic.

Choosing to go without food can be very dangerous. However, that doesn't stop people from fasting for political, religious, or health reasons.

問 1 下線部(ア)の意味として最も適切なものを①〜④の中から 1 つ選べ。

① hurry home
② eat nothing
③ run away from home
④ live and work for nothing

問 2 空所(イ)を満たすものとして最も適切なものを①〜④の中から 1 つ選べ。

① turn
② detail
③ protest
④ competition

問 3 下線部(ウ)が指示する内容として最も適切なものを①〜④の中から 1 つ選べ。

① 選挙権がなかったこと
② 食べ物が十分得られなかったこと
③ 労働環境が悪かったこと
④ 教会で結婚することが許されなかったこと

問 4 下線部(エ)の指示する内容として最も適切なものを①〜④の中から 1 つ選べ。

① some Christians and Buddhists also go to church or temple
② some Christians and Buddhists also fast on special occasions
③ some Christians and Buddhists also work from sunrise to sunset
④ some Christians and Buddhists also take part in volunteer activities

問5 空所（オ）を満たすのに最も適切なものを①〜④の中から1つ選べ。

① food　　　　　② seller　　　　　③ place　　　　　④ medicine

問6 本文の表題として最も適切なものを①〜④の中から1つ選べ。

① Diet and Health　　　　　② Eating Moderately

③ Living in Good Health　　　　④ Reasons for Going without Food

問7 本文の内容と一致するものを①〜⑦の中から3つ選べ。

① We must be physically active to keep extra calories out of the body.

② Mohandas Gandhi did not fast as a political tool.

③ Cesar Chavez fasted for political reasons.

④ Mark Twain believed fasting was a useful way of getting rid of a cold.

⑤ Upton Sinclair used to eat a lot and suffer from stomach troubles.

⑥ People today no longer fast.

⑦ Fasting is dangerous except for patients suffering from medical problems.

9

次の英文を読んで，あとの問いに答えなさい。

Each year on December 10, the world's attention turns to Sweden for the announcement of the Nobel Prize winners. The Nobel Prizes, six prizes given to groups or individuals who really stand out in their fields, were founded by a Swedish inventor, Alfred Nobel.

(ア)Alfred Nobel was the man who invented dynamite, a powerful explosive. During his life, Nobel made a lot of money from his invention, and he decided that he wanted to use his money to help scientists, artists, and people who worked to help others around the world. When he died, his will said that the money would be placed in a bank, and the interest the money earned would be given out as five annual cash prizes.

The prizes set up by Nobel were first handed out in 1901, and included physics, medicine, chemistry, literature, and peace. (イ)Later, in 1968 the Bank of Sweden added a prize in economics to celebrate the bank's 300th year of business.

Each person who receives a Nobel Prize is given a cash prize, a medal, and a certificate. The prize money for each category is currently worth about a million dollars, and the aim of the prize is to allow the winner to carry on working or researching without having to worry about raising money.

The prizes can be given to either individuals or (ウ)groups. Prize winners include Albert Einstein (physics, 1921), Kenzaburo Oe (literature, 1994), Kim Dae Jung (peace, 2001), the United Nations (peace, 2001), and Nelson Mandela (peace, 1993).

The prize winner that has won the most times is the International Committee for the Red Cross. (エ)This

<u>organization</u> has received three Nobel Peace Prizes (in 1917, 1944, and 1963), and the founder, Jean Henri Dunant, was awarded the first Nobel Peace Prize, in 1901.

次の英文①～⑧の中から，本文の内容に一致するものを 5 つ選びなさい。

① The Nobel Prizes are given to people around the world who worked with Alfred Nobel.

② Alfred Nobel was an inventor and set up the Nobel Prizes.

③ In 1901, six Nobel Prizes were first handed out.

④ A prize in economics was later added.

⑤ Nobel Prize winners are given three things that include money.

⑥ Kim Dae Jung, Kenzaburo Oe, and Nelson Mandela are all peace prize winners.

⑦ The International Committee of the Red Cross was founded by Jean Henri Dunant.

⑧ Jean Henri Dunant was one of the first Nobel Prize winners in 1901.

問 2 下線部（ウ）（エ）について下記の質問に文中から答えなさい。

（ウ）groups とありますが，ノーベル賞を受賞した団体を 1 つ英語で書きなさい。

_____

（エ）This organization とありますが，その名前を英語で書きなさい。

_____

問3 賞金の目的が文中に書かれていますが，それは何ですか。簡潔に日本語で説明しなさい。

_____

_____

問4 下線部（ア）（イ）を日本語に直しなさい。

（ア）
_____

_____

（イ）
_____

_____

次の英文を読んで，あとの問いに答えなさい。

Many people don't know that the difference between success and failure is often very small. One does not need to be twice as good, let alone perfect, in order to succeed in most things. In fact, often only a tiny difference separates winners and losers. A small difference may make a big difference. This is true in many areas of life, especially if the small difference is regular and repeated.

For example, consider two clocks, running at a speed differing only by one second per hour. Only one second per hour doesn't seem like much, but it is almost a half minute per day, or almost three minutes a week, or about twelve minutes a month, and almost two and a half hours a year. Well, there's actually quite a difference between those two clocks.

Sports is another good example. One doesn't have to be much better than others to win. The difference between winning and losing is often very small. At the Olympics, the difference between winning and losing is often just 0.1 second or just a centimeter or two. Such a small difference can determine who gets a gold medal.

A small difference, often just a percent or two, if repeated over and over, will almost always lead to success in the future. One does not need to be a genius, does not need to be ten times better, or even twice as good, let alone perfect. Just a small difference is usually enough to succeed.

Our heroes seem to have superpowers, but actually they are just normal people. They are not really that much different from us. They are just a tiny bit faster, or smarter, or more beautiful than average. If one wants to be successful, just remember that the difference between success and failure is often very small. So why don't you try just a little harder, a little more often? A small difference may make a big difference. You may be surprised by the result.

問1 What don't many people know?

① A small success is often different from failure.

② Failure and success are often different.

③ There is often a small difference between success and failure.

④ Failure is often a small success.

問2 A person who wins a gold medal is often someone who _____ .

① is ten times faster

② is twice as fast

③ is just a little faster

④ never gives up

問3 "A small difference may make a big difference" means _____ .

① success often depends on a little luck

② success often depends on small things

③ never give up

④ life is often true

問4 The difference between winners and losers is often _____.

① quite a bit

② a lot

③ twice as good

④ not much

問5 According to the story, _____ usually leads to success.

① being mostly better just a little of the time

② being a lot better most of the time

③ repeating just a percent or two

④ being perfect in the future

問6 According to the story, we can be more successful if _____.

① we are a genius

② we are ten times better

③ we are perfect

④ we are just a little better

問7 Heroes _____.

① have superpowers

② are successful because they are usually a bit better

③ are much different from others

④ are not really more beautiful than average

問8 At the end of the first paragraph, the expression "the small difference is regular and repeated" means _____.

① practice over and over

② a small difference is often just a percent or two

③ a small difference

④ a series of small differences

問9 The word "result" at the end of the story refers to _____.

① your success

② your effort

③ trying harder

④ a small failure

問10 What's the best title for this story?
① Practice Makes Perfect
② A Small Success
③ How to Succeed
④ How Not to Make a Difference

次の英文を読んで，あとの問いに答えなさい。

In the early 1940s, on the night of her graduation party, a high school girl named Doris Van Kappelhoff was involved in a serious car accident. She had planned to go to Hollywood to become a dancer in films, but her injuries made that future no longer possible. During her long recovery at home, Doris began to sing along with the female vocalists on the radio. Her voice became so well trained that she was hired to sing in a band, and soon thereafter, she found parts in movies, changing her name to Doris Day. Her original plans were destroyed by a tragic event, but thereby she found her true calling. Things don't always go according to our plans, but a change of plans may be an example of coincidental circumstances that lead us to a fulfilling life, unguessed and unsought — a blessing from God.

We make plans expecting to be in control of what will happen. Perhaps we fear natural happenings, things turning out contrary to our wishes. The course of life is challenging if we are concerned with trying to control it. We may act with precision, and self-discipline, expecting the world to do the same and give us what we want, but that is rarely the case.

Perfect discipline, or perfect control, is the most certain way to miss out on the joy of life. The unexpectedness of life means that we are free not to plan perfectly. We can flow into the natural chaos of life, so untidy, so unpredictable, or we can try to order life fully by making careful plans. But as Rover Burns says, "The best-prepared schemes often go wrong and leave us nothing but grief and pain for promised joy."

Making plans is an adult occupation, a feature of a

healthy ego. However, life often does not proceed according to our plans. This does not have to leave us disappointed. Perhaps we believe the universe has a plan that more accurately reflects our emerging destiny.

空所に入れるのにもっとも適切なものを選びなさい。

（ア） Doris Van Kappelhoff _____.

① was injured in a car accident on her way to the graduation ceremony

② wanted to act in Hollywood movies in the future

③ gave up becoming a dancer in Hollywood movies

④ was hospitalized for several years

（イ） Doris improved her singing skills by _____.

① singing along with the female singers on the radio

② acting her parts in Hollywood movies

③ being hired to sing in a professional band

④ finding her true calling

（ウ） The author believes we _____.

① are trying to control how other people behave

② can never know completely what will happen in our lives

③ rarely fear things will happen contrary to our wishes

④ should expect the world will give us our reward

(エ) What Rover Burns means is that _____ .

① we can improve our lives if we make the best plans

② we often have to lead a miserable life if we are unlucky

③ even the best plan may lead to a sad and painful end

④ the best plan will prevent us from falling into disappointment

(オ) The best title for this passage is _____ .

① "Life Is Not Always Fair"

② "How to Receive the Feeling of Others"

③ "People Are Not Loving and Loyal All the Time"

④ "Things Do Not Always Go According to the Plan"

次の英文を読んで，あとの問いに答えなさい。

Hunting for a job is a painful experience, but one that nearly everyone must endure at least once in a lifetime. Books are published and magazine articles are written on the subject, all trying to tell job-seekers what they should do or avoid doing （　ア　） to survive and to win the game. They can't calm the nervous applicant (and what applicant is not nervous?), but they do offer some advice that deserves consideration.

To begin with, it is not a good idea to be late. Job interviewers don't think very highly of the candidate who arrives twenty minutes after the appointed time, offering no apology or explaining that he couldn't find the street, and that his watch is slow. The wise job-seeker explores the place the day before to make sure that he can locate the building, the right floor, and the office in which the interview is to take place; at the same time he looks around to see what the employees are wearing and how they seem to behave at work. Next day he arrives early for the appointment. It does not matter if the employer's secretary recognizes him and mentions his first visit to her boss. （　イ　） the eager candidate can only be regarded as smart, thoughtful, and well-organized — three points in his favor before he has said a word.

Most personnel managers admit that they know within the first few minutes of the meeting whether or not they want to hire the person to whom they are talking. This is particularly true when their first reaction to the applicant is negative, when the man or woman has made a disastrous first impression. But what makes a *good* impression? What counts?   Being on time does, as we have seen; then, appearance.   It is (**ウ**) for the candidate to be dressed properly, and to look alert, pleasant, and interested.   It is also very important to look the interviewer in the eyes because this "eye contact" gives a strong impression of sincerity and openness.

問1 本文中の(ア)〜(ウ)に入る最も適切なものを①〜④から1つずつ選びなさい。

(ア) ① in order ② with regard
③ in the end ④ with reference

(イ) ① However, ② What is more,
③ On the contrary, ④ Accordingly,

(ウ) ① formal ② essential
③ genuine ④ valid

(ア)	(イ)	(ウ)

問2 次の(エ)〜(カ)が本文の内容と一致するように，最も適切なものを①〜④から1つずつ選び，英文を完成しなさい。

(エ) Books on hunting for a job _____
① are painful to read.
② list likely employers.
③ make people nervous.
④ give useful guidance.

(オ) Job applicants should _____
① avoid being recognized if they arrive in advance.
② visit the office a day early to avoid getting lost.
③ arrive after the appointed time to be regarded as smart.
④ mention their thoughts about employees' clothing and behavior.

26

(カ) It's important to make a good first impression because _____

    ① managers make their hiring decisions very quickly.

    ② candidates are dressed well and are interested.

    ③ interviewers are impressed by sincere "eye-contact".

    ④ applicants otherwise react negatively.

次の英文を読んで，あとの問いに答えなさい。

Phillis Wheatley was (**ア** bear) in Senegal. She arrived in America on a slave ship around 1761, when she was seven or eight years old, and was purchased in Boston by John Wheatley, who wanted a personal (**イ**) for his wife, Susanna Wheatley. When the Wheatleys' daughter saw Phillis trying to write the alphabet with chalk on the wall, she (**ウ** teach) her to read. (**エ**)Within a year and a half, Phillis was fluent in English and had also begun to study Latin. By the time she was thirteen she was writing poetry. Her work began to appear in New England newspapers, and she became a regional celebrity. She had found a way out of the normal restrictions of her (**オ** assign) role in life through poetry.

(**カ** treat) more as a daughter than a servant by the Wheatley family, Phillis became known for her dignity and conversation as well as her writings. In Britain, the Countess of Huntington admired one of her poems, and arranged the publication of a book by (**キ**)a very extraordinary female slave. The high point of Phillis Wheatley's life came in 1773, when she traveled to England, where she was taken up by the literary celebrities of the day and invited to be presented at court. But the illness of Susanna Wheatley cut short her visit, and Phillis returned to (**ク**), where her mistress died and John Wheatley officially freed her.

She was the first American writer to achieve international (**ケ**). Benjamin Franklin read her work, which sometimes compared the experience of a slave to that of American colonists under British tyranny. George Washington invited her to visit him at his camp during the War of

Independence. Some historians credit her with Washington's decision to allow black men to serve in his army.

Phillis Wheatley found no happiness in her own (コ). She continued to live with her old master until his death, but the people of Boston had much less interest in her as a free black woman than they did when she was the beloved (サ) of a prominent white family.

下線部(エ)を和訳しなさい。

_____

_____

問 2 下線部(キ)は誰を指しているのか，その人物の名前を本文中から探して
書きなさい。

_____

問 3 (ア)(ウ)(オ)(カ)の中の語を適切な形に変えなさい。解答はすべて 1 語
で答えなさい。

(ア)		(ウ)	

(オ)		(カ)	

問 4 空所(イ)(ク)(ケ)(コ)(サ)の中に入るべき文脈上最も適切な語を 1 語選
びなさい。

(イ) ① friend   ② servant   ③ writer

(ク) ① Boston   ② London   ③ Senegal

(ケ) ① fame   ② freedom   ③ journey

(コ) ① activity   ② liberty   ③ slavery

(サ) ① liberated   ② slave   ③ writer

問5 次の①～⑦の中で本文の内容と一致する事柄を述べている文には○，
一致しない文には×を書きなさい。

① Phillis came to America in the mid-seventeenth century.

② Mr. and Mrs. Wheatley had no children and took Phillis as their
own daughter.

③ Phillis was not good at English when she came to America.

④ Phillis worked for New England newspapers.

⑤ The Wheatleys didn't like Phillis very much even though she was a
good servant.

⑥ Mrs. Wheatley freed Phillis on her death bed.

⑦ Some black men fought for the independence of America.

次の英文を読んで，あとの問いに答えなさい。

We've used the wind as an energy source for a long time. The Babylonians and Chinese were using wind power to pump water for irrigating crops 4,000 years ago, and sailing boats were around long before that. Wind power was used in the Middle Ages, in Europe, to （ ア ） corn, which is where the term "windmill" comes from.

The sun heats our atmosphere unevenly, so some parts become warmer than others. These warm parts rise up, other air blows in to replace them — and we feel a wind blowing. We can use the energy in the wind by building a tall tower, （ イ ） a large propeller on the top. The wind blows the propeller round, which turns a generator to produce electricity. We tend to （ ウ ） many of these towers together, to make a "wind farm" and produce more electricity. The more towers, the more wind, and the larger the propellers, the more electricity we can make. It's only worth building wind farms in places that have strong, steady winds.

The best places for wind farms are in coastal areas, （ エ ） the tops of rounded hills, on open plains and in gaps in mountains — places where the wind is strong and reliable. Some are offshore. To be worthwhile, you need an average wind speed of around 25 km/h. Most wind farms in the UK are in Cornwall or Wales. Isolated places （ オ ） farms may have their own wind generators. Several wind farms supply electricity to homes around Los Angeles in California.

The propellers are large, to take energy out from the largest possible volume of air. The angle of the blades can be changed, to cope with varying wind speeds, and the generator and propeller can turn to face the wind wherever it comes from. Some designs use vertical turbines, which don't need to be turned to face the wind. The towers are tall, to get the propellers as high as possible, up to where the wind is stronger. This means that the land beneath can still be used for farming.

問1 （ア）から（オ）に入る最も適切な単語を，次の①〜③の中から選びなさい。

（ア）　① steam　　② grind　　③ peel

（イ）　① of　　② with　　③ towards

（ウ）　① build　　② blow　　③ convert

（エ）　① at　　② in　　③ under

（オ）　① likely to　　② which are　　③ such as

次の①から⑤の英文を読んで，本文に照らして正しいものに〇，間違っているものに×をつけなさい。

① European people were the first to use wind power in agriculture.

② The cause of wind lies in the difference of temperature in some parts of the air.

③ A wind farm is constructed in places where wind is stronger.

④ Most wind farms are situated offshore.

⑤ Vertical turbines turn the generator and propeller to face the wind.

次の英文を読んで，あとの問いに答えなさい。

Growing up without language

It is almost impossible for us to imagine growing up without language, which develops in our minds (ア)so effortlessly in early childhood and plays such a central role in defining us as human and allowing us to (イ)participate in our culture. Nevertheless, being (ウ)deprived of language occasionally happens. In recent centuries children have been found living in the wild, said to have been raised by wolves or other animals and deprived of human contact. It is hard to know the real stories behind these cases, but they are all (エ)strikingly similar with respect to language. The pattern is that only those rescued early in childhood developed an ability to speak. Those found after they were about nine years old learned only a few words, or failed to learn language at all.

One of the most famous of these cases is that of Victor, "the wild boy of Aveyron," made famous in a film by François Truffaut called *The Wild Child*. Victor was captured in 1800, when he was about ten or eleven. He was studied by a young physician named Jean Itard, who creatively and (オ)painstakingly tried to teach him to speak, read, and write. But despite Itard's best efforts, Victor never learned to speak; he learned to read and print only a small set of words.

Children without hearing are not as handicapped. A deaf child can still have language and relate normally to others through signing — (カ)as long as language development starts early. There are a number of studies that show that the sooner a deaf child (キ)is exposed to a natural sign language, such as American Sign Language, the more (ク)proficient a signer he or she will become. As in other cases of linguistic isolation, the ability of deaf people to learn new *words* is not (ケ)affected by the age at which they are exposed to language. But their ability to learn grammar is dramatically affected. Studies of deaf children exposed to sign language after the preschool years show that there is (コ)a critical period for grammatical development, which ends, perhaps, in the early school-age years.

問1 上記英文中の下線部 (ア)〜(コ) の意味内容としてもっとも適切なものを，それぞれ①〜④から 1 つ選びなさい。

(ア) so effortlessly
① so often   ② with so much trouble
③ so easily   ④ with so little reason

(イ) participate in
① play a role in   ② create
③ do well at   ④ teach

(ウ) deprived of
① added to   ② denied contact with
③ led up to   ④ stolen from

(エ) strikingly
① usually   ② very   ③ partly   ④ in no way

(オ) painstakingly

① for a long time   ② innocently

③ in various ways   ④ taking a lot of trouble

(カ) as long as

① while   ② as well as

③ provided that   ④ in the same way

(キ) is exposed to

① shows ② is bought ③ masters ④ has contact with

(ク) proficient

① skillful ② realistic ③ entertaining ④ fortunate

(ケ) affected

① improved ② influenced ③ shown ④ understood

(コ) a critical

① a large ② an open ③ an important ④ a shallow

問2 下記の文章①～⑨の中で本文の内容に一致するものを 3 つ選びなさい（順序は問わない）。

① No child ever misses out on learning a language in order to communicate.

② Language is one of the main things that make us human.

③ Children can start learning a language successfully at any age.

④ After much hard work, Victor learned to speak a few words.

⑤ Itard succeeded in teaching Victor to read a little but not to speak.

⑥ Deaf children are worse off than children isolated from language.

⑦ It's easier for deaf children or children isolated from language to learn grammar than vocabulary.

⑧ Sign language is of no use to deaf children.

⑨ It's essential to learn grammar by a relatively early age.

次の英文を読んで，あとの問いに答えなさい。

A star is a big ball of fire in space that makes lots of light and other forms of energy. A star is mostly made up of gases and something like fire, only much hotter. There are thousands of explosions happening all over the star all the time. This is where the star's heat and light come from. These explosions are also where a star gets its color from.

Our sun is a star. It is the closest star to our planet, and it sends its energy to the Earth as heat and light. The sun seems large to us, but it is only a medium sized star called a yellow dwarf (small star). Other stars can be different colors. Some stars have more energy than our sun and burn even hotter than our sun does. Stars that are hotter than our sun may look blue or white. Stars that are cooler than our sun may look orange or red.

Stars come in many sizes. Our sun is about 1.4 million kilometers around, but people still call it a dwarf because many stars are much bigger. For example, there are many stars which are more than 100 times bigger than our sun. The largest stars are called red supergiants. These stars are so big that most of our small solar system would fit inside one. (ア)If our sun turned into a red supergiant, the outside of the sun would be past Jupiter's orbit.

Stars, just like people, have a life, but a star's life is much longer than a human's life. The sun is millions of years old and will live for many more millions of years. When our sun starts to die, it will grow into a red giant star. (イ)It will not become a supergiant because it is not heavy enough. When our sun dies, it will get so hot that the heat and light will burn the Earth. In fact, it will be too hot for anything to live on the Earth when our sun becomes a red giant. Then, our sun will slowly get darker and colder until it stops giving off any energy at all.

問1 本文の第１段落の内容に合うものとして最も適当なものを, ①～④から１つ選べ。

① Some stars do not have any explosions because they have no gases.

② Stars usually have less than one thousand explosions on their surface.

③ The star's color is not related to the explosions around the star.

④ The star's heat and light are caused by explosions on it.

問2 本文の第２段落の内容に合うものとして最も適当なものを, ①～④から１つ選べ。

① Compared with the sun, stars that look orange are much hotter.

② Stars may look blue when they have a lower temperature than the sun.

③ There are no stars which burn much hotter than the sun.

④ There are some stars which produce more energy than the sun.

問3 下線部(ア)の内容として最も適当なものを，①〜④から1つ選べ。

① If the sun became a red supergiant, Jupiter would be far from the sun.

② If the sun changed into a red supergiant, Jupiter would be inside the sun.

③ If the sun hit a red supergiant, Jupiter would not exist anymore.

④ If the sun went around a red supergiant, it would be close to Jupiter.

問4 本文の第3段落の内容に合うものとして最も適当なものを，①〜④から1つ選べ。

① Dwarf stars cannot be as large as the sun.

② One of the biggest stars in space is the sun.

③ Red supergiants are a type of dwarf star.

④ There are a lot of different-sized stars.

問5 下線部(イ)の内容として最も適当なものを，①〜④から1つ選べ。

① As it gains weight, the sun will slowly grow into a supergiant.

② Because of its weight, the sun cannot be a supergiant.

③ The sun can get as big as a supergiant because it is heavy.

④ The sun will become a supergiant when it loses enough weight.

① After it becomes a red giant, the sun will quickly get cold and dark.

② Creatures on the Earth will survive after the sun becomes a red giant.

③ The sun continues to produce heat and light forever even after it dies.

④ When the sun dies, the temperature of the Earth will get much higher.

問 7 本文の内容に合わないものを, ①〜⑦から2つ選べ。

① The forms of energy that the Earth gets from the sun are heat and light.

② The Earth is heated mainly by the energy produced by a red supergiant.

③ The sun is much bigger than all the other stars called "yellow dwarfs."

④ The temperatures of white stars and red stars are not the same.

⑤ Many stars in space are more than one hundred times the size of the sun.

⑥ The sun is expected to continue to exist for millions of years more.

⑦ The sun can become a giant star but not a supergiant.

MEMO

MEMO

MEMO

MEMO

出題校一覧：
英文 1 ：駒澤大
英文 2 ：専修大
英文 3 ：追手門学院大
英文 4 ：広島国際学院大
英文 5 ：九州国際大
英文 6 ：東京電機大
英文 7 ：亜細亜大
英文 8 ：白百合女子大
英文 9 ：兵庫県立大
英文 10：日本大
英文 11：近畿大